SFO'S PICOT LACE DESIGNS II

MORE NEW LIGHTS ON TATTING AND NEW TWISTS ON BEADING

BY SANDY FORRINGTON

FIRST EDITION

PICOT PRESS, MENDOCINO, CALIFORNIA

SFO'S PICOT LACE DESIGNS II

MORE NEW LIGHTS ON TATTING AND NEW TWISTS ON BEADING

BY SANDY FORRINGTON

Published by:

Picot Press
Post Office Box 2298
Ft. Bragg, CA 95437 U. S. A.
(707) 964-7604

Photography by Gary Betts

Copyright ©1994 by Sandy Forrington, SFO Enterprises & Picot Press
First Printing 1995
Printed in the United States of America

ISBN 0-9642395-2-3

TABLE OF CONTENTS

ACKNOWLEDGMENTS

First of all I would like to acknowledge and pay tribute to Jess Shirley, my photographer for several years, and a joy of a man to work with. He contracted cancer and was gone within three weeks of his diagnosis. He will be sorely missed by all of those whose lives he touched with his gentle and sensitive nature and delightful humor. Thank you, Jess.

As in the first book, I wish to thank my main proofers, Nancy Lamphear and Gleanna Veater, I appreciate their willingness to help me smooth out the rough spots. Also to Diane Mello, my newest proofer who was wonderful!

I regret not having my husband, Cass, play such a large role in the proofing process as he did in the first book, his work schedule does not allow for as intense involvement this time around, but I would like to thank him nonetheless for his ongoing support for my endeavors and the continuing faith and encouragement he gives me. Going from housewife to career woman in such a short space of time has, at times, been a bit unnerving, and he is always there to "soothe my fevered brow".

I would also like to thank Jules and Kaethe Kliot for their ever present patience and support, as well as much appreciated advice and guidance.

I must also give thanks to my children, Cassie and Michelle, who put up with my deadlines and rush orders and trips to the city that are quite boring for them. They keep my spirits high and fuel me with kisses.

Lastly, but not least, as this whole process seems to be a major journey in faith for me, I must thank God, and all those who He puts in my path who help me in innumerable ways, and who are too many to name, but all appreciated.

PREFACE

Here is the second book in, hopefully, a long series of design only PICOT LACE books. I will take the basic technique which was taught in great detail in the first book, and the design shorthand introduced there, and provide you with an ever expanding library of transposed tatting patterns and original picot lace designs.

These design only books are predicated on the assumption that you already know how to do picot lace and how to read the picot lace shorthand. Because all of these designs use the basic technique of picot lace construction and the picot lace design shorthand which were introduced in my first book, PICOT LACE, the basic technique section of this and the subsequent design books is only a schematic condensation of what was elaborated on in the first book.

I do not wish to overcharge or in-sult those who do own my first book by expecting them to wade through many pages of material with which they are already familiar. At the same time, I have endeavored to make this succinct enough for a review.

Keep in mind also that there are more advanced techniques introduced on in the first book which are not elaborated in this book, and that each subsequent design book will contain new advanced techniques which also will be merely illustrated and not elaborated upon in future books. As I begin this series, I would like to make it possible for any book to be owned and worked from, independently of the rest, although I cannot stress strongly enough the recommendation for the first book to be owned as a foundation to the rest. But, beyond that, each book of the series will have a short illustrated section of tech niques previously introduced to enable a quick review by the artist.

If you have purchased this book without either having learned the basic technique or having owned the first book, PICOT LACE, be aware that while picot lace is very easy to do once the basic construction techniques have been learned, it is a little tricky to develop the rhythm. It took 75 pages in the first book to elaborate on the technique and help the student to work through to a comprehension of the technique, and although this process only takes a few hours, it is the foundation of all that will be introduced in these design only books. If you do not understand the picot lace shorthand, you will be handicapped when you attempt an intricate piece because the graphics and the directions are intended to complement one another and to fill in the inevitable gaps each is bound, by its very nature, to leave.

So, in conclusion, if you have bought only this book, and find yourself at a loss for comprehension, or find yourself confused, please do not curse me, but resign yourself to going back and learning the proper foundation which was presented in the first book, which was designed to instruct so thoroughly that most any picot lace design can then be tackled.

As I move through the process of transposing more and more tatting patterns, I am constantly having to create new technique variations to enable you to execute the designs. Again, those will be presented in each book in such a way that those with the proper foundation will be able to understand the summary presented, even if the elaboration of that technique was in a previous, design only book. Enjoy the rhythm!

CHAPTER 1

GETTING STARTED

If you are picking up this book for the first time, and are not familiar with the picot lace technique, it is important that you read the preface.

If you have worked your way through the first book, PICOT LACE, welcome again. As I move into the design series of picot lace books, I will be introducing to you new techniques appropriate to the designs included here. In the basic technique section you will find a review of the basics and the more advanced techniques introduced in PICOT LACE. This review is intended to merely refresh your memory of what you have previously learned, although if you are reading Design Book 2, and have not purchased Design Book 1, the review provided should still, with your basic knowledge in tact from the first book, be adequate for comprehension. My goal here is to make the design only series both self contained and affordable, as well as interesting, and not redundant.

I will also include in this chapter a reiteration of some of the better tips and new discoveries introduced in the Picot Lace Newsletter, which at the time of this publication is still free to all those who own the first book. I only ask that you send a Self Addressed Stamped Envelope to help defray postal costs. This review of tips, etc. I do also with an eye towards the time when the mailing list is too large to be able to continue to do it this way, and a nominal subscription fee must be charged.

So, knowing that some of your tips may end up here, please continue to send them in, they increase the richness of the picot lace experience for us all, enabling new design heights to be reached.

In the first book, I mentioned that one should never use picot beads larger than their base beads. I also advised never to use beads smaller than 11°. The former was advice passed on from several of my technical advisors. I have since found that while generally this is true, you don't want to put a 10° bead on a small czech 11° bead, but if the size difference is not that large, say a Japanese 11° as the picot on a small czech base bead, it will probably work just fine. The latter advice was based upon my own experimentation with Czech beads. With a personal stash of over $2,000 worth of beads, I had slowed down in my purchases, and since I live in an area where there is no bead store, I was not aware as that book went to print that the Japanese had been busy with other beads than the Delicas. They have produced some wonderful new beads with very large holes which enable even their 14° or 15° (seems they are the same although called differently by different suppliers,

so I have been told), to work beautifully for use in picot lace. The simultaneous blessing and drawback of the 15° beads is that they produce a piece that is approximately 30% smaller than the same piece made in 11° beads, and so to do a length of picot lace for a trim, neckband, or bracelet will take you 30% more time, but of course, it has a far daintier effect too. The 11° beads out of Japan are a bit larger than the czech 11°, my main supplier feels that they are actually closer to being a 10.5°. There are also some gold lined beads coming out of Japan that are quite exquisite, but may be difficult to find as not all suppliers are carrying them.

As with the czech beads, you do want to steer clear of the Japanese two cuts, make sure the beads you choose have well tumbled edges, as you will be tweaking down alot with your Type B thread and do not want the piece to break either as you work on it, or later. A few times, I have succumbed to a particularly luscious shade of square cut bead, felt pleased with myself when I completed it with no thread breaks, only to pull it out at a show and discover that the thread had been cut after it was completed! And while it is possible to reconstruct and thus salvage a piece, it is frustrating nonetheless.

I did find, quite accidentally, that once completed, when a piece breaks, it will not fall apart. My 6 year old daughter caught a chain edge of a bracelet I had given her on something and broke the thread. That was nearly a year and a half ago, and it has traveled with me to countless shows and classrooms, and has only lost about 4 or 5 beads, the chain is still in tact!

Alice Korach, in her forward in the first book, PICOT LACE, made mention of my intent to publish the third book on how to transpose your own tatting patterns. At the time I mentioned that intent to her, I was still reading through the tatting instruction and making a sometimes not so logical jump, but now I think, breathe, and dream picot lace in such a way as to not only confound those intentions, but to drive my husband crazy when he wants to go to bed, and all I want to do is bead some more! Now I only look at the tatting pattern and, for the most part, with some admitted trial and error, make an intuitive jump as to the transposition process required. I have discovered in my increasing teaching experience, that the basic rings, loops and chains I have introduced for picot lace are easily translated into tatting. That is to say, if you see a loop in tatting with 3 picots on it, odds are great that it is an 8/3 loop, and if the bottom is longer, that is, the loop sits higher than most, it is most likely a 10/3. I try, in my classes to impart some of what is involved in the transposition process, but I have not yet come to the point where I have determined how to write it down clearly enough to be understood. As you experience the designs, you too will see.

GLOSSARY

This section illustrates all the standard loops and chains most commonly used in picot lace. Rings always have the picots spaced evenly around them.

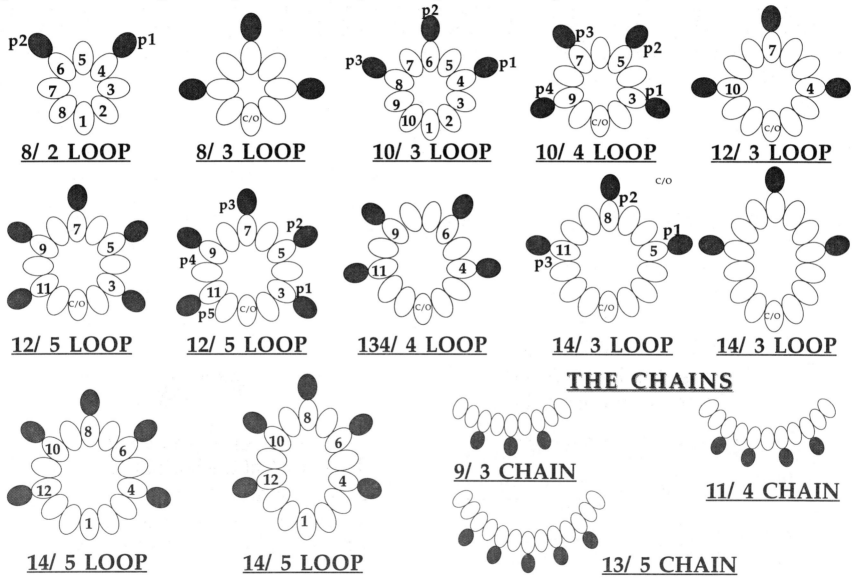

8/ 2 LOOP **8/ 3 LOOP** **10/ 3 LOOP** **10/ 4 LOOP** **12/ 3 LOOP**

12/ 5 LOOP **12/ 5 LOOP** **134/ 4 LOOP** **14/ 3 LOOP** **14/ 3 LOOP**

THE CHAINS

14/ 5 LOOP **14/ 5 LOOP** **9/ 3 CHAIN** **11/ 4 CHAIN**

13/ 5 CHAIN

CHAPTER 2

BASIC TECHNIQUE

Whenever possible here, I have merely illustrated the basics and not provided more than the most rudimentary definition. This is part of the effort to maximize space and keep printing costs to a minimum, to keep your cost down.

BASIC TERMS

bb—base bead
Any non-picot bead.

꒕꒕꒕꒕꒕꒕꒕꒕꒕꒕꒕꒕꒕꒕

p—picot
The beads which sit upon the base beads—ALWAYS a different color from the bbs.

꒕꒕꒕꒕꒕꒕꒕꒕꒕꒕꒕꒕꒕꒕

Ch—chain
That which connects 2 loops.

C—Center
꒕꒕꒕꒕꒕꒕꒕꒕꒕꒕꒕꒕꒕꒕

𝓁 —loop
Note the lack of a picot at the bottom of the loop; the ⊕ bead is your crossover bead. A loop ALWAYS has a crossover bead.

꒕꒕꒕꒕꒕꒕꒕꒕꒕꒕꒕꒕꒕꒕

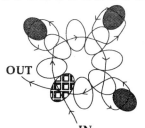

c/ o—crossover bead.
That bead, at the bottom of a loop, through which the thread goes in 2 opposite directions (shown as ⊕). Always counted as bb #1 in a loop.

R—ring

A ring has no chain attached, no c/o bead, and the picots are evenly spaced.

Motif

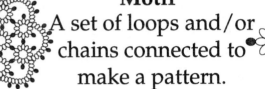

A set of loops and/or chains connected to make a pattern.

sep—separate or separated.

join

To connect to an existing part by its preset picot: ⊛.

p on 3rd bb

Picot on that numbered bead⊛ (could be any number).

sp—spacer bead.

That bead which is placed between any number of closely set loops. Shown as ⊛.

medallion

A motif with border, or borders around it.

p on 3rd, 5th, and 7th bb

Picots on those numbered beads (could be any number).

1 2 3 4 5 6 7 8 9

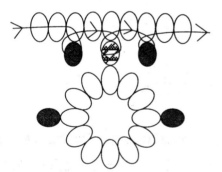

border

An edging for a motif, medallion, or series of motifs. Usually most easily accomplished by running a chain, locking into the top picots of the loops as you go.

CHAPTER 3

BASIC TECHNIQUE REVIEW

Again, this is merely a schematic condensation of the techniques elaborated upon in the first book. If any of these are not easily understood, please refer to the extensive graphic and verbal explanations provided in the first book, PICOT LACE for further clarification.

THE PICOT MOUNT

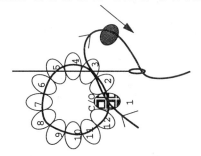

Use a backward motion with your needle after making a single pass through a loop to secure loop. Chain picots are mounted as you make the chain. On a first loop or on a ring, make two passes through before mounting any picots. The c/o bead is always bead #1.

TYING OFF & ON

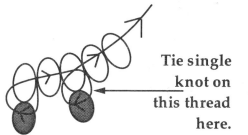

Tie single knot on this thread here.

Tie a single knot at a picot junction. Tie off on 2 or 3 consecutive picots, go through 4 more base beads and snip. Tie on the same way, with 2 or 3 knots, preferably in a chain.

JOINING

To join, simply lock into the preexisting picot instead of mounting a new picot, with the same backward motion used in all picot mounts.

JUMPING

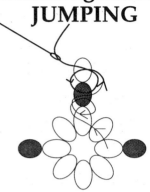

When you jump, you are merely mounting a base bead on top of a picot. This base bead becomes a bead in the loop, ring, or chain you are jumping into.

THE SECOND LOOP

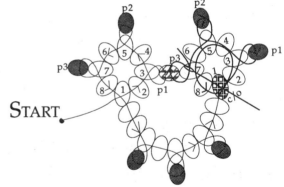

1st loop threads are simplified for clarity. Note the first picot on the 2nd loop is the one farthest away from the 1st loop, and how the 2nd loop joins on its third picot to the 1st loop, to position you for the next chain from the c/o bead.

THE LAST LOOP

The last loop in a circle joins, or locks into, the picots on either side in order to complete the circle, as shown by the highlighted beads.

THE SPACER BEAD MOTIF

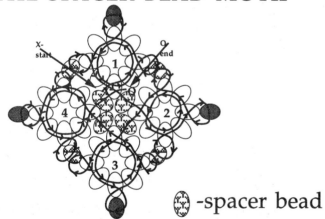

-spacer bead

This shows the anatomy of a motif with spacer beads. Trace the thread passage with you finger to understand the circular motion which is used in all picot lace, and feel the rhythm therein.

THE CLOVERLEAVES (CLVF)

There are 3 types of Cloverleaf:

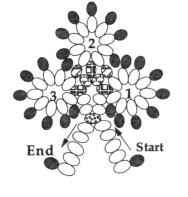

Open Cloverleaf:
Clvfs always have spacer beads. The 1st loop is on the starting side, and the two chains are joined as you leave the Clvf.

Closed Cloverleaf:
In this Clvf, a bb from the entering chain is reentered upon exiting. As in the first Clvf, the first loop is on the side you start from.

Closed, Reverse Clvf:
In this Clvf, a bb from the entering chain is reentered upon exiting, also. But, the 1st loop is the one on the far side of the Clvf. This makes it sit more horizontally than #2.

PICOT LACE SHORTHAND

In the designs, you will find 12/6Rs and 10/3 ᘒ, as well as 13/5 Chs. In all of these cases, the first number refers to the number of bbs and the second to the number of ps. The examples above are all standards, a graphic list of which you will find in the glossary in Chapter 4. Any deviation from the basic standards will be noted as indicated in the basics, p on bb #3, 4, and 5 for example.

Joining is indicated by where and what number the p would be if it were a new one. Remember the flow and that the 1st p of a loop is mounted on the far side from where that loop will join its previously made neighbor.

Again, the design shorthand is elaborated upon in the first book, and is only reviewed here. The following symbols are used in all books:

◯—base bead   ⬭—special function bead

⬯—c/o bead   ⬯—joining picot

⬬—picot bead   ⬯—spacer bead

CENTER FILLER STRIP

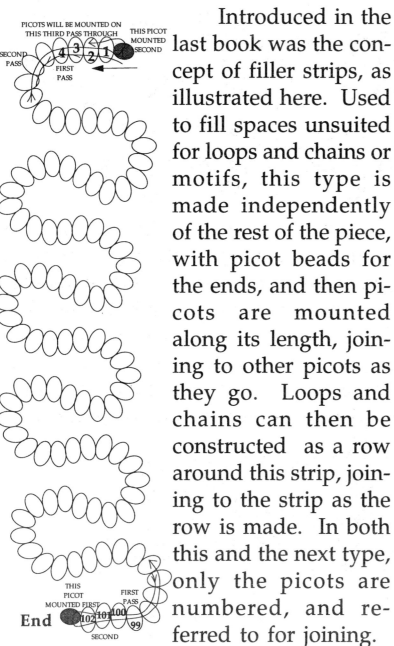

PICOTS WILL BE MOUNTED ON
THIS THIRD PASS THROUGH

THIS PICOT
MOUNTED
SECOND

4 3 2 1

SECOND
PASS

FIRST
PASS

THIS
PICOT
MOUNTED FIRST

FIRST
PASS

End 102 101 100 99

SECOND

Introduced in the last book was the concept of filler strips, as illustrated here. Used to fill spaces unsuited for loops and chains or motifs, this type is made independently of the rest of the piece, with picot beads for the ends, and then picots are mounted along its length, joining to other picots as they go. Loops and chains can then be constructed as a row around this strip, joining to the strip as the row is made. In both this and the next type, only the picots are numbered, and referred to for joining.

NEW TECHNIQUES

Here the concept of filler strips is elaborated upon, this type I call a filler strand, because the strip is made as a chain, not premade as in the center filler strip. In the center filler strand, the surrounding motifs are set in place, then the center filler strand is made as a chain which joins to the motifs and to itself as it is constructed.

In both cases, for simplicity in reading, only the picots are numbered and made reference to for joining to and from other ps, and, as in all picot lace, the picots are mounted as soon as possible.

This means that, as shown on the next page, that while picot #7 is shown as a connecting picot, it is set on new as #7, and joined to when you come around to #11.

The concept of filler strips and strands is really fairly simple once you actually get to doing it, I have illustrated the picot count on both the strip and the strand on the next page for clarity.

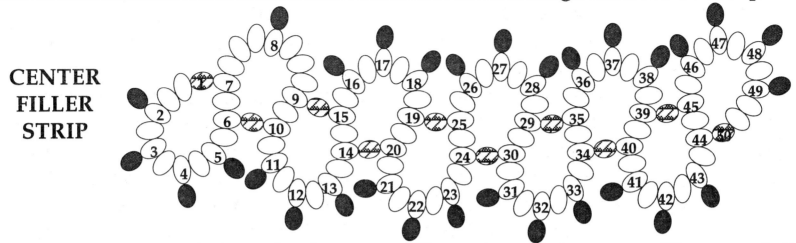

CENTER FILLER STRIP

Here they are, side by side, the center filler strip and the center filler strand. Both of these graphics are modified from their design originals for clarity and comprehension. As you can see, only the picots are numbered, and, in both examples, p6 is mounted as a new picot, and then when you get around to p10, you join to the p6 you previously mounted. The strip has a picot bead at either end of the chain, whereas the strand starts out of a special function bead and ends in a picot on a neighboring motif. The strand is placed after the surrounding motifs are constructed, whereas the strip is made first, and then will have a row placed around it of loops and chains.

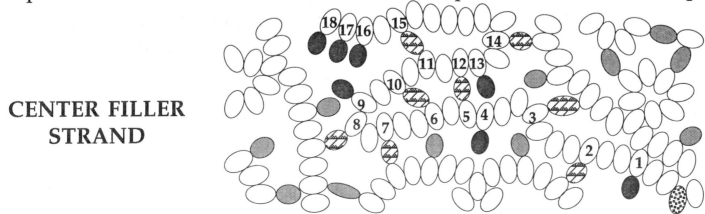

CENTER FILLER STRAND

NEW TECHNIQUES

THE SWEEPING ROW

This is a condensation of Figs. 10-13 of this collar design, and is used in the case of rows around a motif that intersect on another. When this sweep is used, a base bead in the chain around the motif becomes a c/o bead for the second sweep. By doing two sweeps or rows in this fashion, bulky joints are eliminated and the rows create a more fluid motion around the motif.

The best way to do this is to jump out of the motif, rather than starting a new thread. For stability, jump out in such a way as to move to the inside on this first sweep, where you join to the other picots close in.

You are weaving from the inside to the outside as you ring the motif. Two sweeps complete the two rows, but neither is an inner or an outer because of the weaving.

This is the same graphic as Fig. 13, but with the thread passage shown.

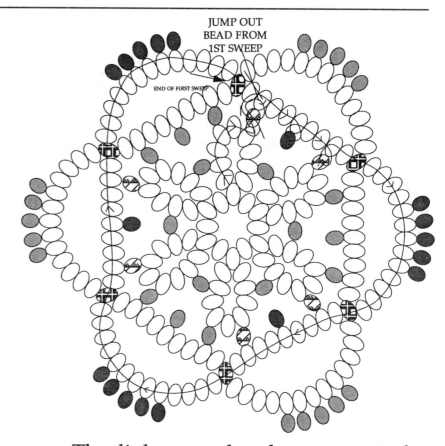

The light grey beads represent the picots in the 2nd sweep around. The c/o beads are, in this sweep, only bbs of the chains, they will become c/o beads on the 2nd sweep. At the end of this sweep, you will pass on to the next c/o bead before starting the 2nd sweep, and it will start on the inside, just as this 1st sweep did, but on the next section over.

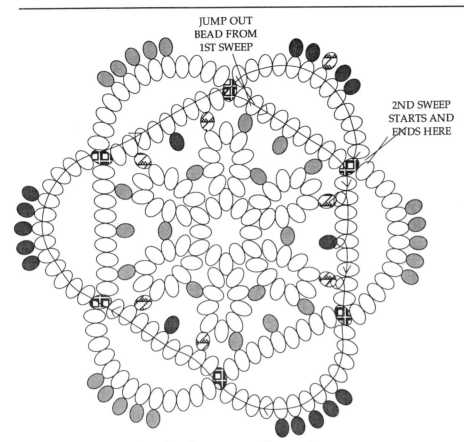

JUMP OUT
BEAD FROM
1ST SWEEP

2ND SWEEP
STARTS AND
ENDS HERE

Here, the light grey beads represent the picots in the 1st sweep around. The c/o beads are now used to pass through the 1st row to do another section of the 2nd row. On the last section of this sweep, in the collar design, the 3rd picot joins to the center motif of the heart medallion, make sure you do not mount a new picot!

LOCKING DOWN

Now, I am of the opinion that most anything is possible, even if not in coventional ways.

It was as a result of this opinion that when I made this motif with the sweeping rows and it buckled a bit with the beads I was using, that I decided the solution to the problem would be to lock down the center picot of the inner sweeps. This may not be necessary for you, depending upon what beads you are using, and there are probably other ways to accomplish this, but this way worked for me, and so I pass it on to you.

By locking down the middle picot of the inner sweeps to the connecting picot of the center motif, it is pulled away from the outer sweeps, and secured so that the buckling is eliminated.

It does make the entire motif much tighter, and depending upon the beads you are using, this may or may not be desirable. The next page shows detailed graphics of the lock down.

Here is the motif with two sweeping rows around it, and the center picots of the inner sweeps locked down. As you can see the center picots are locked down in a perpendicular fashion to the picots which join the loops of the spacer bead motif that was the start of this whole thing. Much of the makings of this expanded motif comes under the heading of, "rules are meant to be broken."

Normally, you would not have 4 beads coming out of a c/o bead as when the sweeping rows cross, and rarely do you see two picots placed perpendicular to one another. But this latter method can also be used for inserting larger beads into a piece. The next page shows a close up of how to lock down.

I have split this into two graphics to more clearly show the lock down process. You enter the middle picot as you would in a picot mount, then enter the picot joining the loops which sits below and perpendicular to it, as shown in Fig. 1, below. You then tie off on one of the picot edges there and return into the middle picot of the inner sweep. Swing around through the base bead and reenter the middle picot from the opposite side, and then the perpendicular picot, as shown in Fig. 2. Tie off as before, on the picot edge, reenter the middle picot, and exit via the base bead, and go around to the next one and repeat. This example starts from the right and goes left.

FIG. 1   FIG.2

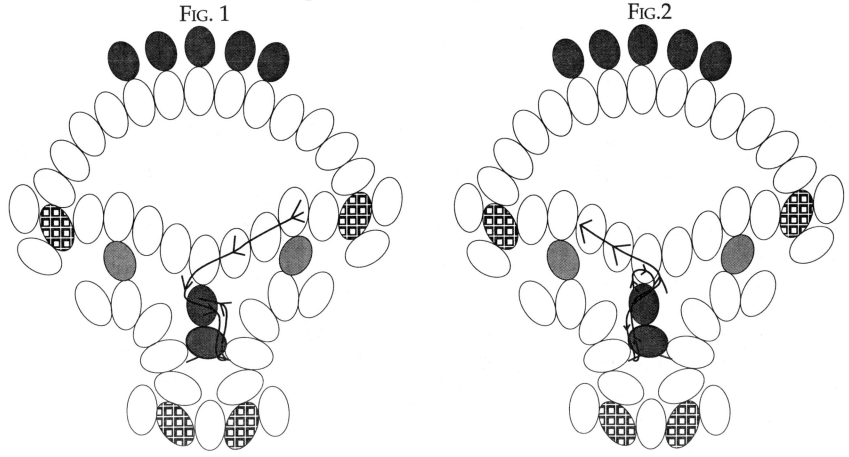

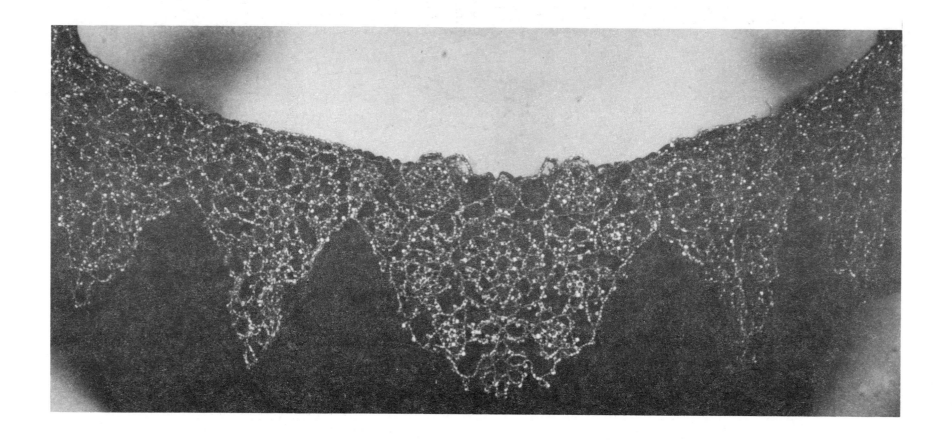

THIS OFF-THE-SHOULDER COLLAR IS MADE UP OF **21** IDENTICAL SMALL MEDALLIONS AND ONE LARGE HEART MEDALLION FOR THE CENTER, AND IS MOUNTED UPON ELASTICIZED LACE FOR VERSATILITY. DEPENDING UPON THE FINISHED SIZE COLLAR DESIRED, YOU MAY WISH TO USE MORE OR FEWER OF THE PLAIN MEDALLIONS. TRY IT ON FOR SIZE AS YOU CONSTRUCT THE MEDALLIONS. WHILE THE COVER SHOWS THE COLLAR IN ITS ENTIRETY, HERE IS A CLOSE UP OF EACH OF THE TWO DIFFERENT MEDALLIONS USED.

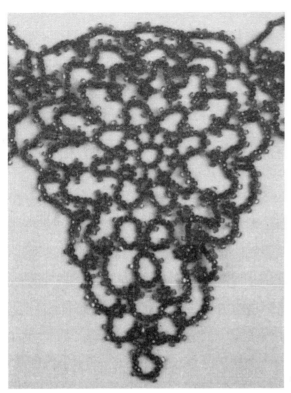

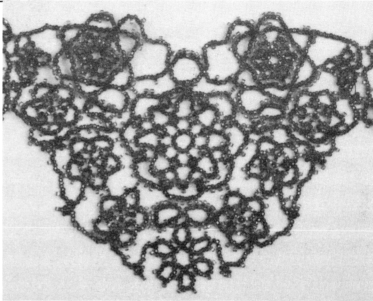

DEW DROP COLLAR

   This collar consists of two separate types of medallion, the first, I call the plain medallion, and multiples are made of it. They are attached as they are made, and when all the desired ones are finished, an edging is placed around the top to prevent the top from flopping over. The heart medallion is made up of 4 distinct motifs which are connected as they are worked, and then filler strands are added to tie it all together. This center medallion is connected to plain medallions, one on each side. This final connection is done at the last stage of the construction process and is accomplished by extending the top edging to connect with the heart medallion, and then making the other required connections.

   The directions given here are designed to compliment and clarify the graphics provided. It is not recommended that you follow either one, the graphics or the directions exclusively, but rather that you use the two concurrently. While I recommend a cursory perusal of both, do not be dismayed if either one seems overwhelming. Not only are they designed to be worked through, but they are an extremely advanced design. You should do fine if you just move along step by step and study the graphics carefully.

THE PLAIN MEDALLION

Start with a 16/8 R. **See Fig. 1.**

Jump out from any p and make an 8/3 ℓ. ** Then make a 13/5 Ch. Make a second 8/3 ℓ, joining p2 to the next p of the R as you go around, and p3 to p1 of the previous ℓ worked. Repeat from **, remembering that on the last ℓ, p1 will join to p3 of the 1st ℓ made and p3 will join to p1 of the previous ℓ. Finish with the last 13/5 Ch by reentering the c/o bead of the 1st ℓ. Tie off. **See Fig. 2.**

With a new thread, make a Cloverleaf (Clvf) of three, 20/5 ℓs, ps on bbs #5, 8, 11, 14, and 17, using 1 sp. bead. To do this and make the proper connections, I suggest this order. Do the 1st ℓ complete. This will be your bottom ℓ of the Clvf. On the 2nd ℓ, join p2 to p2 of any one of the Chs on the motif you just made. On the 3rd ℓ, join p2 to p2 of the next Ch over on the completed motif. **See Fig. 3.**

First row of medallion: Now, you can tie off, or jump from the 2nd p of the 1st ℓ after you finish the Clvf. Either way, make an 8/3 ℓ which joins to p2 of the 1st ℓ made in the Clvf.

If you have jumped, you will be going around the motif and Clvf in a clockwise direction. If not, set up your ℓ such that you are so you can easily follow these directions.

Coming out of this ℓ, make a 13/5 Ch and go into another 8/3 ℓ. You make your way around the motif and Clvf, all the ℓs will be 8/3 ℓs and all the Chs will be 13/5 Chs. The connection points for the 16 ℓs are shown in the graphic, Fig. 4—I list them here by #.

#1. Join p2 of ℓ to p2 of 1st Clvf ℓ made.

#2. Join p2 of ℓ to p4 of 2nd Clvf ℓ made.

#3. Join p2 of ℓ to p4 of same Ch 2nd Clvf ℓ was joined to.

#4. Join p2 of ℓ to p3 of next Ch up, going clockwise.

#5. Join p2 of ℓ to p2 of next Ch up.

#6. Join p2 of ℓ to p4 of same Ch as #5 joined to.

#7 & 8; Same as #5 and # 6 on next Ch up, over, or down as you

#9 & 10; proceed around motif and Clvf in a clockwise direction.

#11 & 12.

#13. Join p2 of ℓ to p3 of next Ch.

#14. Join p2 of ℓ to p2 of next Ch. (This Ch also connects to Clvf.)

#15. Join p2 of ℓ to p4 of 3rd Clvf ℓ.

#16. Join p2 of ℓ to p4 of 1st Clvf ℓ.

Construct last chain or row and finish by reentering c/o bead of 1st ℓ of this row. For simplification purposes, tie off now. **See Fig. 4.**

Second and last row of medallion: Start with an 8/2 ℓ, ps on bbs #3 & 5, but add no new ps! Rather, join p1 to p5 and p2 to p1 of the 2 adjacent Chs of #13 ℓ of 1st row—bear with me, there is a reason I'm having you start here. As you work around each medallion, you will be able to connect to the neighboring medallion on your last 2 Chs by beginning here and moving in a clockwise direction.

All the ℓ in this row are 8/2 ℓ, but all the Chs are not all13/5 Chs, so don't get ahead of yourself. As in the 1st row, the connection points for the 18 ℓ are listed here by #. **See Fig. 5.**

Remember, your last 2 Chs will connect to the medallion you have just finished. Even though you will have nothing to connect your 1st medallion to, the connection directions below WILL include those connections. Fig. 5 is counterclockwise.

#1. Join p1 of ℓ to p5 of Ch leading into #13 ℓ of 1st row and join p2 of ℓ to p1 of Ch leading out of #13 ℓ of 1st row. Ch, 13/5.

#2. Join p1 of ℓ to p5 of Ch leading into #14 ℓ (same Ch as last p was joined to), and join p2 of ℓ to p1 of Ch leading out of #14 ℓ. Ch, 13/5.

#3. Straddle 2 Chs in the same manner as #1 ℓ and #2 ℓ did, moving clockwise. Ch, 13/5.

#4. Straddle 2 Chs in the same manner as #3 ℓ. Ch, 9/3.

#5. Place new p as p1. Join p2 to p2 of Ch leading out of #16 ℓ of 1st row. Ch, 25/5, ps on bbs #5, 9, 13, 17, and 21.

#6. Join p1 to p4 of same Ch coming out of #16 ℓ of 1st row and join p2 to p1 of #5 ℓ of this row. Ch, 9/3.

From here through #17 ℓ, all Chs are 13/5s and all ℓ straddle 2 Chs in the same manner as ℓ # 1 through 4 did.

After leaving #17 ℓ, join p4 to matching p of neighboring medallion.

After leaving #18 ℓ, join p3 to matching p of neighboring medallion. **See Fig. 6.** Lay out your work frequently to keep your orientation correct.

Top edging row of medallions—*to be done after all desired medallions are complete.* Begin above #13 ℓ of 2nd row around medallion for simplification. **See Fig. 7.**

In the same manner in which you constructed 8/2 ℓ and 13/5 Chs for the 2nd row of the medallion, straddling the Chs leading into and out of the ℓ of the 1st row of the medallion,*** join 8/2 ℓ to #16 through #13 ℓ of 2nd row of medallion, placing a 13/5 Ch between each set of ℓ. Come out of the #13 ℓ with a 13/5 Ch and then construct a Clvf.

The Clvf which sits between each set of two medallions is made up of three, 10/4 ℓ, w/1 sp bead on each loop. The 1st ℓ straddles #12 ℓ on ps 2 and 3 (p2 joins to p5 of Ch leading into #12 ℓ and p3 joins to p1 of Ch leading out of #12 ℓ). The 2nd ℓ of the Clvf joins on p2 to p3 of the Ch leading into #18 ℓ of the far medallion (the p just above the one which connects the 2 medallions). P3 of this 2nd ℓ of the Clvf joins to p3 of the Ch leading out of #11 ℓ. P4 joins to p1 of the 1st ℓ of the Clvf. The 3rd ℓ of the Clvf joins on p2 to p1 leading out of #17 ℓ of the neighbor medallion. P3 of this 3rd Clvf ℓ joins to p5 of Ch leading into #17 ℓ of the neighbor medallion, and p4 joins to p1 of 2nd Clvf ℓ. Leaving the Clvf, join p2 of this next 13/5 Ch to p4 of the Ch you made coming into the Clvf. Repeat from *** until you have edged all of your medallions. **See Fig. 8.**

THE HEART MEDALLION

For this center piece, the heart medallion, you will construct 4 different motifs, a different number of each, and connect them as you go.

Center motif: Start with the same center motif you made for the plain medallions. That is, around a 16/8 R, place eight, 8/3 🟣 and 13/5 Chs. **See Figs. 1 and 2.** Ring this with 8/2 ls and 13/5 Chs, straddled as in the medallions. **See Fig. 9.**

Top, medium motifs: Start the two, top, medium motifs by first constructing a spacer bead motif consisting of six 10/4 🟣, w/1 sp bead. To do this, make a 10/4 ℓ, **then set on 11 bbs and close the ℓ on the last 10. This puts your sp bead into its proper position. The 2nd ℓ of this sp bead motif will join on p4 to p1 of the previous ℓ. Repeat from ** until you set on the last ℓ. This last ℓ joins by p1 to p4 of the 1st ℓ worked, and by p4 to p1 of the previous ℓ worked. Add 1 more sp bead and your spacer bead motif is done and ready for the 2 sweeps that ring it. **See Fig. 10.**

The 1st sweep is made by first jumping out of any designated picot (2 or 3) of the sp bead motif. **See Fig. 11.**

This ring is constructed as a continuous Ch. So, from the jump, set on ***3 bbs w/p on bb3; 3bb join bb3 to closest p on next ℓ over. **See Fig. 11.**

Now set on 7 bbs w/p on bb7. The next 4 bbs all have ps on them. Set on 7 more bbs, joining bb 7 to the p on the far side of the next ℓ over. **See Fig. 11.**

Repeat from *** until you are ready to join the Ch to the jump out bead. Your piece should now look like Fig. 11.

For your 2nd sweep, in the graphic, I lightened up the 1st sweep for clarity. In this and the last graphic, Fig. 11, you'll notice the highlighted c/o beads—they are just ordinary bbs, but now on this 2nd sweep, they will be employed as c/o beads. From where you reentered the jump out bead, proceed to the nearest c/o bead—that is the 2nd bb over from the jump out bead. **See Fig. 12.**

Now do this sweep in much the same fashion as you did the 1st sweep, with only a couple of differences. So, here we go.

****From the c/o bead, set on 2 bbs, join bb2 to the next p on a ℓ en route. **See Fig. 12.**

3 bbs, p on bb3; 3 bbs, join to p on next ℓ over; set on 1 more bb and go through c/o bead (second bead over towards you from the next p over). **See Fig. 12.**

Out of this c/o bead, set on a 13/5 Ch w/ps on bbs #4, 5, 6, 7, and 8. End this Ch by entering the next c/o bead (the 2nd bb over from the 1st p attached on the 1st sweep). **See Fig. 12.**

Repeat from **** until you prepare to set on your 3rd and last 13/5 Ch. On this one, on the 3rd p of this Ch, you will join to the center motif you have made and set aside. This one is marked in the graphic as a special joining picot. Finish this Ch and reenter the c/o bead you started this sweep with. Tie off. **See Fig. 13** for completed view.

The specially hightlighted beads on the 2 sweeps are so noted to provide you with the visuals necessary should you choose to lock them down into the center connecting picot beads directly beneath them. This locking down is accomplished by entering the highlighted picot bead, then entering the center connecting picot bead which is perpendicular to the 1st. Tie off on an edge on the far side of the connecting picot and reenter the 1st. **See Fig. 14** for an overview of the heart medallion with the center and two, top, motifs completed.

Small, side motifs: Each of these six, small side motifs will be connected to other motifs as it is being constructed, and some connections that you may think should be made will not be made now, but will be filled in later by the filler strands. **See Fig. 16** for an overview of the motif with all six of these small, side motifs in place.

So, to start, make five, 8/3 ℓℓ and 9/3 Chs, joining each ℓ to the next. That is, make an 8/3 ℓ and a 9/3 Ch. On the 2nd ℓ join p3 to p1 of the previous ℓ. Join ℓs in this fashion as you go around. On the last ℓ, join p1 to p3 of the 1st ℓ and p3 to p1 of the previous ℓ. On the last Ch, going clockwise, join p1 to p5 of the next Ch out from where the top, medium motif joins the center motif, and join p3 to p1 of the next Ch out on that top, medium motif. **See Fig. 17.**

Now jump into any one of the p2s and cinch together all 5 of these in the center and as best you can (choose any 2 of the picot beads to go back and forth between), set a bb into the center with a figure '8' motion. **See Fig. 15.**

The 2nd of these six, small, side motifs will join by p3 of its last Ch, going clockwise, to p3 of the next Ch down from the top, medium motif on the center motif. **See Fig. 18.**

The 3rd motif will join by p3 of the 4th Ch, again going counter clockwise, to p1 of the 2nd Ch worked of the 2nd motif. **See Fig. 19.**

Also join p2 of the last Ch of this motif to p3 of the next Ch down on the center motif. **See Fig. 20.**

Now, we'll place a double loop below the center motif and between the 2 lowest, small, side motifs.

These double loops are each 20/16 ℓs and their c/o beads are cinched together in the same way as jumps are made. For cohesion and ease of working strength, I suggest you make a ℓ of 20, 'jump' out of the c/o bead into the other ℓs' c/o bead, make the 2nd ℓ, return then to the 1st ℓ and mount your ps as follows. Your ps will be on bbs # 3, 5, 6, 7, 8, 9, 10, 11, 12, 13, 14, 15, 16, 17, 18, and 19.

P1 joins to p2 of the bottommost Ch of the center motif, moving in a clockwise direction. P2 of your 1st ℓ of the double ℓ joins to p1 of the same center Ch. P8 joins to p2 of the 1st Ch on the 3rd small side motif. All other ps are new. **See Fig. 21.**

Repeat this process on the 2nd ℓ of your double ℓ, in reverse, since you'll be going in the opposite direction. That is, place new ps on bbs #3, 4, 5, 6, 7, and 8, join p9 to p2 of 1st Ch worked on small side motif, new ps on bbs # 10, 11, 12, 13, and 14, p15 joins to p5 of bottommost chain of center motif and p16 joins to p4 of the same center motif chain. **See Figs. 21 & 22.**

Bottom center motif: This last motif you'll need for this heart medallion is also a spacer bead motif and it will be placed under the double ℓ you just made. It consists of six, 15/4 ℓs w/ 2 sp beads, each ℓ connecting to its neighbor.

To do this one, make a 15/4 ℓ, ps on bb #4, 7, 10 and 13. **See Fig. 23.**

Set on 17 beads and close the ℓ on the last 15. This next ℓ joins on p4 to p1 of the previous ℓ. Continue on around in this fashion. On the last, sixth ℓ, going clockwise, join p1 to p4 of the 1st ℓ worked, p2 will join to p2 of the #2 ℓ of the double ℓ, p3 to p15 of the #1 double ℓ, and p4 will join to p1 of the last ℓ worked. **See Fig. 24.**

The filler strands: Move back into ℓ #1 of this sp bead motif you just finished. Come out just past the 1st p, tie off and double back the other way into the same ℓ, coming out between the 2 bbs at the very top between ps 2 and 3. Set on 14 bbs and close a ℓ on the last 6 of these. This will be a 6/1 ℓ. Exit, and make a 12/2 Ch, ps on bb #4 and 8, the p on bb #8 joins to the Ch on the 3rd motif below and to the outside of the one which joined to the double ℓ on its p3 going counterclockwise. **See Fig. 25.**

At the end of this Ch, enter the c/o bead of the ℓ to the outside of the Ch you just joined to. The last bb of this Ch is highlighted as a sp bead because there is not enough room in the c/o bead of that ℓ for six strands to gracefully flow through, so this last Ch bead will act as a sp bead.

After entering the c/o bead, immediately reenter this last Ch bead and begin your new Ch. This 3rd Ch is a 16/2 Ch w/ps on bbs #7 and 12, but the p on bb7 is not a new one, but rather join here to p2 of the next Ch on the small 3rd motif, still going counterclockwise. The count for this Ch begins with the 1st new bb you add. **See Fig. 26.**

ℓ, 6/1. For the moment, ignore the bead highlighted as a special purpose bead, I'll explain in a moment. Ch, 9/1, p on bb #5. Again, use the last bb of this Ch as a sp bead and enter the ℓ of the 2nd small motif that is to the right and to the outside of the Ch which connects to the 3rd small motif. **See Fig. 27.**

Again, immediately reenter the Ch you just made until you have backtracked through 8 bbs. **See Fig. 28.**

Now begin a new Ch. This is why this bead, technically bb #2 of the Ch you just made is highlighted as a special purpose bead.

Your new Ch count begins with the 1st bead you set on of the new Ch. It is an 18/3 Ch, with ps on bb #5, 9, and 14. The p on bb #9 is NOT a new one, rather it joins to p2 of the Ch on the 2nd small motif just up in a counterclockwise direction from the ℓ you just butted the last Ch up against. **See Fig. 28.**

ℓ, 6/1, joining to p1 of the next Ch up from the last Ch you joined to. **See Fig. 29.**

Set on 7 bbs and close the ℓ on the last 6, making it a 6/1 ℓ. For the present time, disregard the highlighted special purpose bead, it will be used to start a new filler strand which will snake between the 1st and 2nd small, side motifs. Out of this last 6/1 ℓ made, Ch, 9/1, p on bb #5. End this Ch in the ℓ which sits directly opposite the Ch of this 1st motif that joins to one of the two top, medium motifs. **See Fig 31**, and also the overview in **Fig. 24.**

Again, this last Ch bead is a spacer type bead and should be immediately reentered. **See Fig. 30.**

Ch, 16/3, ps on bbs #6, 11, and 13. P1 is not new, but joins to p2 of the next Ch up on this 1st small, side motif. **See Fig. 31.**

ℓ, 6/1. Now set on 7 bbs and close ℓ on the last 6, making a second 6/1 ℓ which joins to p2 of the next Ch up. Now, inward on this 1st small side motif, moving counterclockwise, Ch 7/1, p on bb #5.

Now you'll make a closed Clvf. This Clvf is three, 10/3 ℓↄ w/1 sp bead. But being closed means that 2 additional bbs go on the Ch before you start the 1st Clvf ℓ. One of these will become a sp b and the other a c/o bead when you finish this Clvf. **See Fig. 32.**

The 1st ℓ of the Clvf has all new ps. The 2nd ℓ joins on p2 to p5 of the Ch that joins the 1st small, side motif to the top, medium motif; that is, the highest, outermost Ch which is already joined to that 1st small, side motif, and p3 joins to p1 of the 1st ℓ of this Clvf. **See Figs. 32 and 24.**

The 3rd ℓ of this Clvf joins on p1 to p placed on the Ch leading into the Clvf and p3 to p1 of the 2nd ℓ of this Clvf. Leaving this 3rd ℓ. set on 1 bb and reenter the next to last, or bb #8, of the last Ch worked; now this bb is a c/o bead. **See Fig. 33.**

Ch, 20/2, ps on bbs # 3 and 9, where p1 joins to p3 of the 1st ℓ of Clvf, and p2 joins to p2 of the 1st ℓ of Clvf. This Ch, you will note in Fig. 34 has a highlighted special purpose bead at the very end and butts into p3 of the next Ch up, going counterclockwise. As you end the Ch, enter p3 of the medium motif and then double back into the Ch you first constructed and go all the way back down to the highlighted special purpose bead mentioned in Fig. 30; tie off en route for added insurance and security. **See Fig. 34.** Repeat on other side.

This next section, that in Fig. 35, of the filler strand was a graphic nightmare!! Usually if it works in beads, with some finagling it can be made to work on paper. This one was just too much of a stretch, with too many separate parts to deal with. So that it could be followed visually I was able to lighten the parts already constructed and in place and use the darker ink to help you focus on this strand and the connections it makes. Now is when you will need to put blinders on and take this one step at a time. Basically, this section is just a Ch, or a filler strip that you make in place, that begins just after you go through the single bead which sits between the 6/1 ⚭, and is designated on the graphic as a special purpose bead. **See Fig. 35. Also see Fig. 43 for an overview of the entire heart medallion.**

I've numbered where the ps go to make following along easier.

#1. 2 bbs w/p #1 on the third bb.

#2. 3 bbs, join to p2 of Ch of 2nd small, side motif connecting to 6/1 ⚭ at start.

#3. 2 bbs w/p on the second bb.

#4. 2 bbs, join to p3 of 1st small, side motifs' 1st Ch. We're going counterclockwise and this is the Ch just down from where this 1st small, side motif locks into the top, medium motif. **See Figs. 35, 36, and 43.**

#5. 3 bbs w/p on third bb.

#6. 3 bbs w/pon third bb.

#7. 3 bbs, join to p2, going counterclockwise, of 2nd small motif, that is, the p just up from where this 2nd motif locks into the center motif.

#8. 2 bbs, join to center motif on p just above p locking 2nd motif into center motif.

#9. 1 bb w/p.

#10. 1 bb w/p.

#11. 1 bb w/p.

#12. 1 bb w/p.

#13. 1 bb w/p.

#14. 2 bbs w/p on second bb.

#15. 1 bb w/p.

#16. 2 bbs, join to p1 of Ch p4 of this filler Ch joined to on 1st, small, side motif.

#17. 2 bbs w/p on second bb.

#18. 1 bb w/p.

#19. 2 bbs, join to p4 of chain of top, medium motif, going counterclockwise, that 1st small, side motif connects to (the bottommost Ch of that top, medium motif).

#20. 2 bbs w/p on second bb.

#21. 1 bb w/p.

#22. 2 bbs, join to p13 of this Ch.

#23. 1 bb w/p.

#24. 1 bb w/p.

#25. 1 bb w/p.

#26. 1 bb w/p.

#27. 1 bb, join to p1 of Ch on center motif where 2nd small, side motif joins its p2.

#28. 5 bbs, join to p1 of next Ch in on top, medium motif, the same Ch that locks the top, medium motif to the center motif, again moving counterclockwise.

Lock this last bead of this filler strand down like a jump off bead is locked. Tie off and repeat on the other side. **See Figs. 35, 36, and 43.**

The top, center filler strands: Now the last filler strands go at the top, above the center motif and between the top, medium motifs, and consist of 2 strands that cross.

For this one, start a new thread in the top Ch of one of the medium motifs, moving towards the center. Go through the c/o bead and begin your top strand. Again this will be a straight Ch. Let's try this one a new way, similar to tatted instructions. If I write '4 bbs, p', that means place a p on the 4th bb. Again, I will number the picots. So,

1.   4 bbs, p.
2.   3 bbs, p.
3.   3 bbs, p.
4.   4 bbs, join to p3 of 1st Ch in and down from your starting point. **See Fig. 37.**
5.   5 bbs, p.
6.   5 bbs, p.
7.   10 bbs, join to p1 of center motifs' uppermost Ch, moving counterclockwise.
8.   1 bb, p.
9.   1 bb, join to p3 of same center motif Ch.
10. 1 bb, p.
11. 1 bb, join to p5 of same center motif. **See Fig. 38.**
12. 10 bbs, p.
13. 5 bbs, p.
14. 5 bbs, join to p3 of inside Ch of top, medium motif. **See Fig. 39.**
15. 4 bbs, p.
16. 3 bbs, p.
17. 3 bbs, p, 3 bbs and enter the c/o bead of the other top, medium motif which is at the top, inside corner.

As with the other beads highlighted as spacer beads in similar positions, enter the c/o bead and immediately reenter Ch, traveling completely through it to your starting point. When you get there, enter the c/o bead from the opposite side you originally entered, go back into Ch again and tie off.

Lower strand of top, center filler strands: Now enter the Ch at the bottom innermost Ch of the top, medium motif and jump out of its p5. This jump out bead is highlighted as a special purpose bead. **See Fig. 40.**

Set on 9 new bbs. Enter the 5th bb down from p6 on the 1st Ch. This is now a c/o bead.

1. 4 bbs, join to p6 of 1st Ch.
2. 1 bb, p.
3. 1 bb, p.
4. 1 bb, p.
5. 1 bb, p.
6. 1 bb, p.
7. 1 bb, join to p12 of 1st Ch. 3 bb, go through the 5th bb down from p12 of the 1st Ch. This is now a c/o bead. **See Fig. 41.**

Set on 10 bbs and jump from the 10th bb to p5 of the bottom, innermost Ch of top, medium motif. **See Fig. 42.**

To join heart medallion to plain medallion: On your endmost plain medallion, where the top edging ends, set a new thread. Come out of the last c/o bead of the last ℓ and make a 13/5 Ch. Go into an 8/3 ℓ, but place the ps on bbs #2, 4, and 6. None are new. P1 joins to the 1st free p at the top edge of the heart medallion. **See Fig. 44.**

P2 joins to p1 of the Ch leading out of #17 ℓ of the 2nd row around the plain medallion. **See Fig. 7 if necessary.**

P3 joins to p5 of the ch leading into #17 ℓ of the 2nd row around the plain medallion.   **Again, see Fig. 7 if desired.**

Go completely around ℓ again and jump out of p3—you *will* be going the wrong way.

Tie off on the next p (p4) of the Ch you jumped into and double back.   Go to the next Ch and join the bb just after p5 to the uppermost 6/1 ℓ of the heart medallion. **See Fig. 44.**

Go down to the next Ch.   Join the bb *between* ps 1 and 2 to lock into the highest of the final 2 free ps on the matching, adjacent Ch of the heart medallion.   Join the bb between ps 3 and 4 to the last free p on the heart medallion and jump into the heart medallion at that same point.

Now, moving up, lock in p2 of the plain medallion to the matching bb on the heart medallion Ch, and p3 of the plain medallion to the bb next to the top, already locked in, p.   **See Fig. 44.**

Move up past the two 6/1 ℓs into the next Ch.   On bb #5 of this Ch, lock into p3 of the plain medallion Ch opposite you.   Moving through the c/o bead of the closed Clvf, lock in bb #3 to p2 of the plain medallion.   **See Fig. 44.**

Tie off as you head on towards the top of the heart medallion.   I recommend going *all* the way into the top, medium motif and tying off again for strength.   **Finally, Fig. 45** shows the plain and heart medallions connected.

The heart medallion could be used alone to embellish an evening bag or adorn a garment.   One plain medallion without the connecting edging, and with a narrow beaded strand, say of alternating loops, makes a beautiful neckpiece.   You could put fewer of them together and use the edging, leaving out the heart medallion to make a collar that comes up closer to the neck.   You may even choose to leave off the last row to make the medallions more shallow so the weight of the glass would be less.

FINISHING

When I finished mine, I initally intended to simply sew hooks along the top, and eyes along my garment(s) to enable me to wear it with the most versatility, like I do with the classic collar from the first book. But it would not hang properly, the weight of the glass was too much.

So, instead, I mounted it on a six inch deep strip of black lace which had a straight top and scalloped bottom. It took me many tries to get it just right and if I ever get really skinny, it may need to be redone!

I wanted mine to hang off the shoulder as in the cover photo; I first found some clear, thin elastic, the new stuff is amazingly strong and put it around my shoulders to the desired tautness. I then basted it onto the lace, and then pinned the collar to the lace. It did not work because I had not taken into account the weight of the glass beads. So, make your elastic about 2 inches shorter than what feels like the desired tautness, and then baste as indicated above. If it now fits properly, first stitch the elastic to the lace, and then, stretching out the lace to full length as you work, stitch the collar onto the lace.

Make sure you let the collar sit about one quarter to one half inch above the top edge of the lace to prevent the elastic from showing.

If you have carefully measured the lace to the same length as the collar, allowing for the lace seam, and stretch the lace out as you work, the gather created both in the lace and in the collar will be minimal and attractive.

To wear, I just slip it over my shoulders after donning a strapless bodysuit, and I am ready to go. The collar can also be rested upon the shoulders for a more conservative, almost Spanish look.

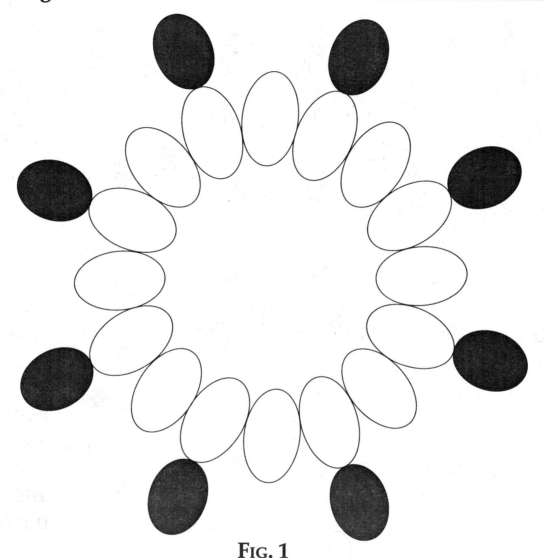

FIG. 1

YOUR FIRST STEP IN CREATING THE MEDALLIONS THAT COMPRISE THE BULK OF THIS COLLAR IS TO MAKE A 16/8 RING. THAT IS, 16 BASE BEADS WITH 8 PICOTS MOUNTED AT EVEN INTERVALS.

IN ALL OF THE GRAPHICS FOR THESE MORE COMPLEX DESIGNS, YOU WILL SEE THAT ONLY THE SECTION BEING CURRENTLY CONSTRUCTED HAS ITS KEY BEADS HIGHLIGHTED TO SIMPLIFY THINGS.

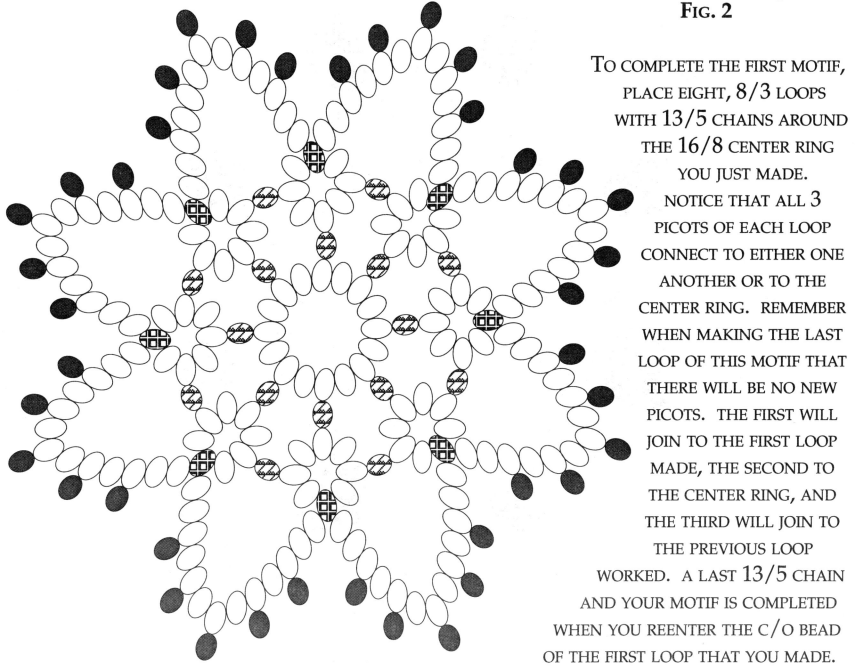

To complete the first motif, place eight, 8/3 loops with 13/5 chains around the 16/8 center ring you just made. Notice that all 3 picots of each loop connect to either one another or to the center ring. Remember when making the last loop of this motif that there will be no new picots. The first will join to the first loop made, the second to the center ring, and the third will join to the previous loop worked. A last 13/5 chain and your motif is completed when you reenter the c/o bead of the first loop that you made.

FIG. 3

NOW YOU WILL PLACE A CLOVERLEAF AT THE BOTTOM OF THE MOTIF YOU JUST COMPLETED. THIS CLOVERLEAF IS MADE UP OF THREE 20/5 LOOPS, EACH LOOP SEPARATED BY A SPACER BEAD. THERE ARE NO CHAINS COMING INTO OR OUT OF THIS CLOVERLEAF. THE TWO TOP LOOPS WILL JOIN TO THE MOTIF, BUT NOTICE THAT THE LOOPS OF THE CLOVERLEAF DO NOT CONNECT TO ONE ANOTHER.

THE DIRECTIONS SUGGEST YOU START A NEW THREAD FOR THE CLOVERLEAF TO REDUCE THE BULK YOU ARE DEALING WITH.

IT DOES NOT MATTER TO WHICH MOTIF CHAIN YOU FIRST JOIN UP WITH, JUST MAKE SURE THAT YOU ARE CORRECTLY PLACED FOR THE LAST LOOP TO JOIN TO THE NEXT CHAIN OVER.

C/O (CROSS OVER) BEAD —

SP (SPACER) BEAD —

JOINING PICOT —

FIG. 4

THE FIRST ROW OF THE MEDALLION COMPLETELY ENCIRCLES BOTH THE MOTIF AND THE CLOVERLEAF ATTACHED TO IT.   IT CONSISTS OF 8/3 LOOPS AND 13/5 CHAINS.

TO BEGIN THIS ROW, YOU MAY EITHER JUMP OUT OR BEGIN A NEW THREAD AFTER TYING OFF THE OLD. IN EITHER CASE, BEGIN THIS ROW SO THAT YOUR FIRST LOOP IS POSITIONED THE SAME WAY AS THE #1 LOOP HERE IS POSITIONED, AND THAT YOU WILL LEAVE HEADED IN THE SAME DIRECTION AS IN THIS GRAPHIC. IN THIS MANNER, YOU CAN MORE EASILY FOLLOW ALONG WITH THE WRITTEN AND GRAPHIC INSTRUCTIONS. LAY IT OUT BEFORE JOINING THE FIRST LOOP TO THE CLOVERLEAF TO MORE EASILY DO THIS. NOTE THAT NONE OF THE LOOPS IN THIS FIRST ROW JOIN TO ONE ANOTHER, THEY ALL CONNECT ONLY TO THE CENTER, ALREADY CONSTRUCTED SECTIONS.

FIG. 5

#14 ℓ #15 ℓ
#13 ℓ #16 ℓ
#12 ℓ #17 ℓ
#11 ℓ #18 ℓ
#10 ℓ #1 ℓ
#9 ℓ #2 ℓ
#8 ℓ #3 ℓ
#7 ℓ #4 ℓ
#6 ℓ #5 ℓ

WHEN YOU COMPLETE THIS SECOND ROW, YOU WILL HAVE COMPLETED THIS MEDALLION. I SUGGEST THAT YOU START THIS ROW WITH A NEW THREAD SO THAT YOU CAN MORE EASILY FOLLOW THE DIRECTIONS WHICH INCLUDE HOW TO CONNECT ONE MEDALLION TO THE NEXT, SOMETHING YOU WILL NOT NEED ON THIS FIRST ONE, BUT WILL BE IMPORTANT ON THE SUBSEQUENT ONES.

NOTICE THAT THIS ROW, WHILE BEING MADE UP OF ALL 8/2 LOOPS HAS THREE DIFFERENT SIZES OF CHAINS. AT THE BOTTOM OF THE MEDALLION, YOU WILL USE TWO 9/3 CHAINS, AND ONE 25/5 CHAIN. ALL OF THE REST OF THE CHAINS ARE 13/5S.

TAKE NOTE ALSO OF THE FACT THAT THE TWO LOOPS AT THE VERY BOTTOM DO NOT STRADDLE TWO CHAINS AS DO THE REST OF THE LOOPS. A COMMON ERROR IN THIS ROW IS TO DOUBLE BACK UPON YOURSELF AND JOIN THE SECOND ROW TO THE SECOND ROW, SO BE AWARE OF YOUR CONNECTIONS AND DO NOT GET CARRIED AWAY WITH YOURSELF AS I DID, SEVERAL TIMES.

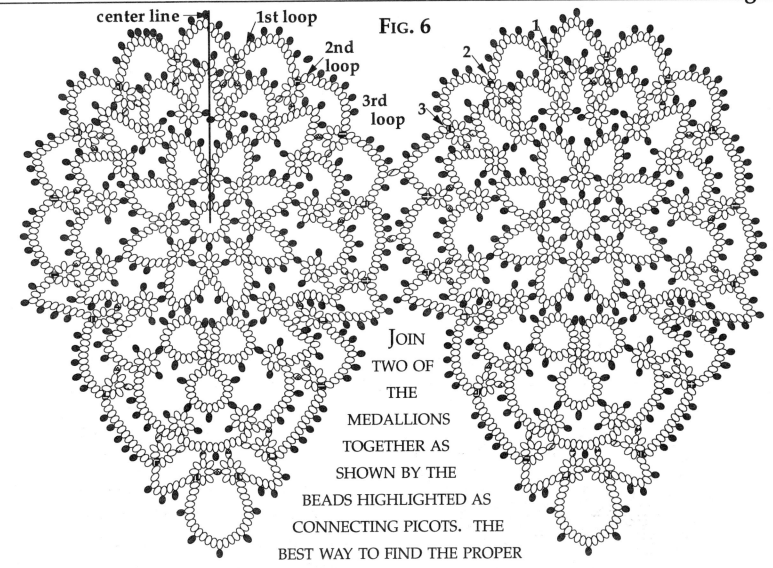

center line →   1st loop

FIG. 6

2nd
loop

3rd
loop

1

2

3

JOIN
TWO OF
THE
MEDALLIONS
TOGETHER AS
SHOWN BY THE
BEADS HIGHLIGHTED AS
CONNECTING PICOTS. THE
BEST WAY TO FIND THE PROPER
CONNECTION POINT IS TO VISUALIZE A CENTER LINE COMING UP FROM THE CENTER RING, AND THEN
COUNT OVER 3 LOOPS. THE FIRST 2 CHAINS AFTER THAT THIRD LOOP ARE THE 2 CHAINS WHICH JOIN TO
THE NEXT MEDALLION. MAKE SURE YOU CLOSELY MONITOR YOUR PROGRESS ON THE LAST ROW OF EACH
MEDALLION SO AS NOT TO MISS THIS IMPORTANT CONNECTION.

FIG. 7

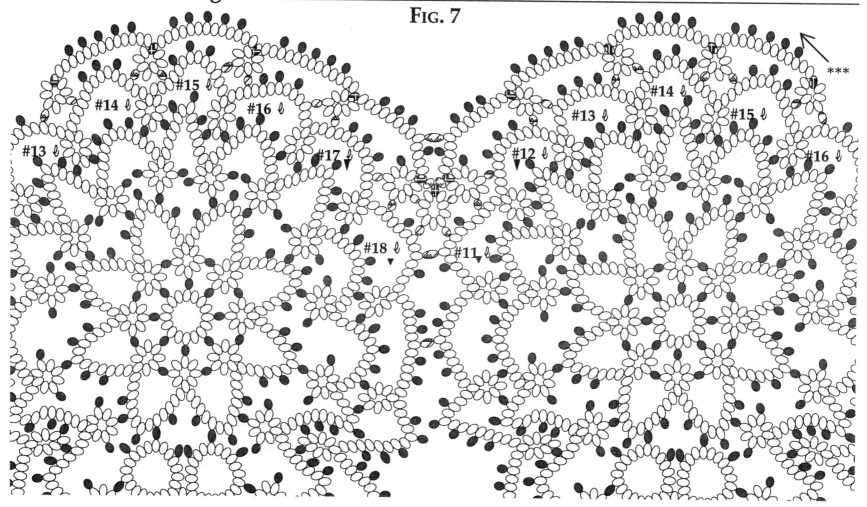

HERE IS THE TOP EDGING WHICH TIES TOGETHER THE MEDALLIONS. JOIN THIS EDGING TO THE 2ND ROW OF EACH MEDALLION BY THE DESIGNATED PICOTS. THE CLOVERLEAF BETWEEN THE MEDALLIONS IS MADE UP OF THREE 10/4 LOOPS, WITH 1 SPACER BEAD. THE CLOVERLEAF LOOPS JOIN TO EACH OTHER, AS SHOWN. REPEAT THIS EDGE UNTIL ALL MEDALLIONS HAVE BEEN JOINED BUT STOP BEFORE BEGINNING ANOTHER CLOVERLEAF WHEN YOU REACH THE POINT WHERE THE HEART MEDALLION JOINS THESE MEDALLIONS. THE END OF THE EDGING IS DIFFERENT THERE, AS YOU WILL SEE LATER.

THE FIRST

LOOP OF

THE NEXT

CLOVERLEAF

WILL

START

HERE

***

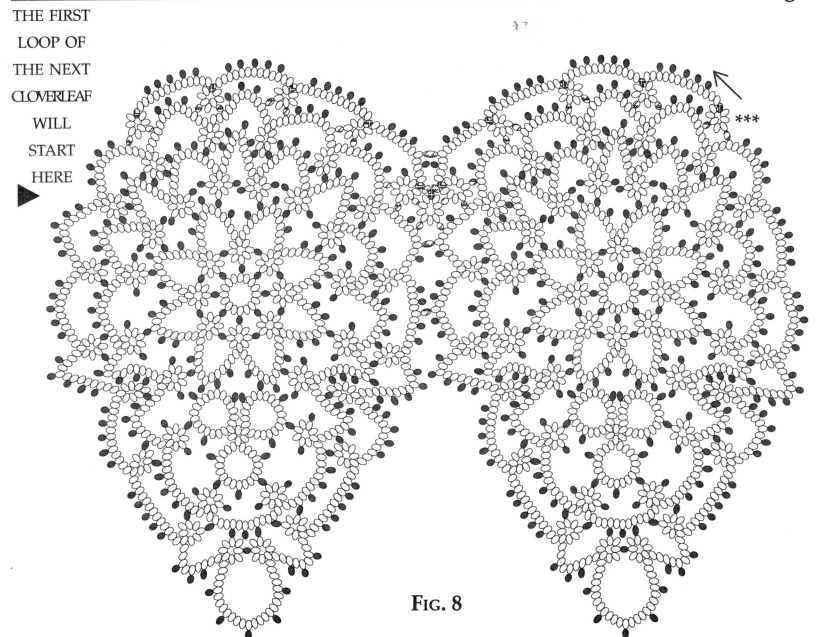

FIG. 8

HERE IS THE SAME EDGING GRAPHIC FROM A SLIGHTLY DIFFERENT PERSPECTIVE.

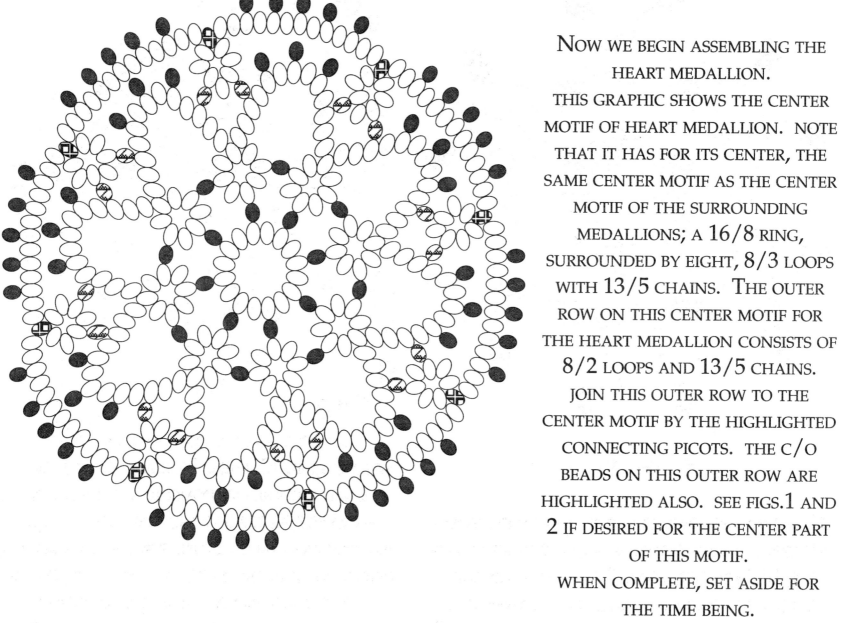

FIG. 9

NOW WE BEGIN ASSEMBLING THE
HEART MEDALLION.
THIS GRAPHIC SHOWS THE CENTER
MOTIF OF HEART MEDALLION. NOTE
THAT IT HAS FOR ITS CENTER, THE
SAME CENTER MOTIF AS THE CENTER
MOTIF OF THE SURROUNDING
MEDALLIONS; A 16/8 RING,
SURROUNDED BY EIGHT, 8/3 LOOPS
WITH 13/5 CHAINS. THE OUTER
ROW ON THIS CENTER MOTIF FOR
THE HEART MEDALLION CONSISTS OF
8/2 LOOPS AND 13/5 CHAINS.
JOIN THIS OUTER ROW TO THE
CENTER MOTIF BY THE HIGHLIGHTED
CONNECTING PICOTS. THE C/O
BEADS ON THIS OUTER ROW ARE
HIGHLIGHTED ALSO. SEE FIGS. 1 AND
2 IF DESIRED FOR THE CENTER PART
OF THIS MOTIF.
WHEN COMPLETE, SET ASIDE FOR
THE TIME BEING.

FIG. 10

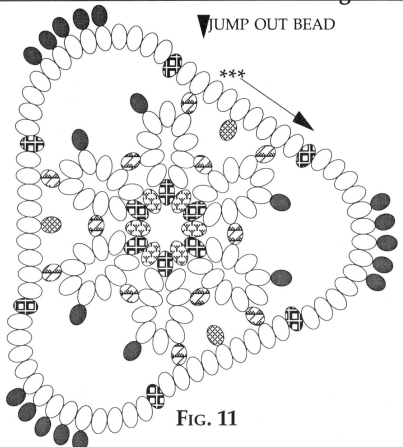

JUMP OUT BEAD

***

FIG. 11

NOW FOR THE TWO TOP, MEDIUM MOTIFS. START THESE WITH A SPACER BEAD MOTIF CONSISTING OF SIX, 10/4 LOOPS, USING 1 SPACER BEAD. THE SPACER BEADS, C/O BEADS, AND CONNECTING PICOTS ARE HIGHLIGHTED AS INDICATED IN FIG. 3

THIS FIRST SWEEP AROUND LOOKS PRETTY STRANGE, HUH? THE C/O BEADS THAT SEEM TO NOT BELONG ARE ORDINARY BEADS WHICH WILL BECOME C/O BEADS WHEN YOU BEGIN YOUR SECOND PASS AROUND THE SPACER BEAD MOTIF. THE BEADS MARKED WITH THE NEW PATTERN ARE LOCK DOWN BEADS, AND THAT OPTION IS EXPLAINED IN THE DIRECTIONS AND IN FIG. 13.

FIG. 12

START HERE ON YOUR 2ND SWEEP. THIS MEANS YOU WILL COMPLETE THE 1ST SWEEP

BY REENTERING THE JUMP OUT BEAD AND THEN GO TO NEAREST C/O BEAD. SO YOUR FIRST SEGMENT OF THE 2ND SWEEP WILL BE A 13/5 CH, THE LAST OF WHICH WILL CONNECT TO THE CENTER MOTIF. IN THIS GRAPHIC YOU ARE GOING COUNTER CLOCKWISE.

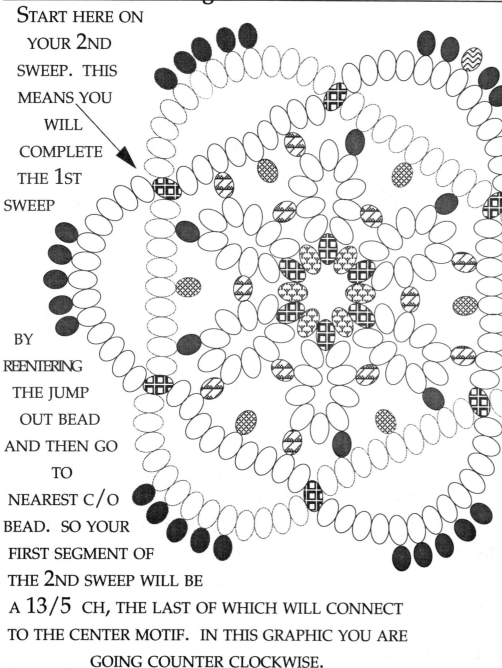

IN THIS GRAPHIC YOU WILL NOTE THAT THE ENTIRE 1ST SWEEP THAT YOU MADE IN FIG. 11 IS NOW A LIGHTER SHADE. THIS SHOULD MAKE IT EASIER FOR YOU TO KEEP YOUR ORIENTATION. YOU CAN SEE THAT THE C/O BEADS FROM THE 1ST SWEEP ARE BEING UTILIZED NOW. AS YOU COMPLETE THIS 2ND SWEEP, STOP WHEN YOU GET TO THE BEAD ON THE LAST OUTER CHAIN MARKED LIKE THIS: ⊛ . IT CONNECTS TO THE CENTER MOTIF. THE FIRST OF THESE TWO TOP, MEDIUM MOTIFS CAN JOIN TO THE CENTER MOTIF AT ANY CENTER PICOT OF ITS OUTER CHAIN. THE SECOND MUST JOIN TO THE CHAIN WHICH IS THE SECOND ONE OVER TO EITHER THE RIGHT OR TO THE LEFT OF THIS ONE. SEE FIG. 13.

FIG. 13

 — SPACER BEAD

 — C/O BEAD

 — CONNECTING PICOT

 — SPECIAL JOINING PICOT

HERE IS THE TOP, MEDIUM MOTIF COMPLETE. ON MINE, I LOCKED DOWN TO THE PICOT BENEATH IT, THE BEAD HIGHLIGHTED AS THIS:  . MY MOTIF BUCKLED A BIT, AND SO I LEAVE THIS AS AN OPTION, YOURS MAY NOT BUCKLE DEPENDING UPON THE BEADS YOU USE. IF YOU DECIDE YOU WANT TO LOCK DOWN THIS INNER RING, GO INTO THE LOCK DOWN BEAD AS IF YOU WERE GOING TO JUMP AND THEN ENTER THE PICOT BENEATH IT. ONCE THROUGH, TIE OFF ON THE PICOT EDGE THERE, AND REENTER THE LOCK DOWN BEAD FROM THE OPPOSITE SIDE YOU LEFT IT. DO THIS PROCESS TWICE, TYING OFF ONCE ON EACH SIDE OF THE PICOT BELOW BEFORE RETURNING THROUGH IT AND BACK INTO THE LOCK DOWN BEAD. SEE PAGE 21 FOR SPECIFIC GRAPHICS ON LOCKING DOWN.

THIS SHOWS THE CORRECT PLACEMENT OF THE TWO, TOP, MEDIUM MOTIFS AROUND THE CENTER MOTIF
OF THE HEART MEDALLION.

FIG. 14

FIG. 15

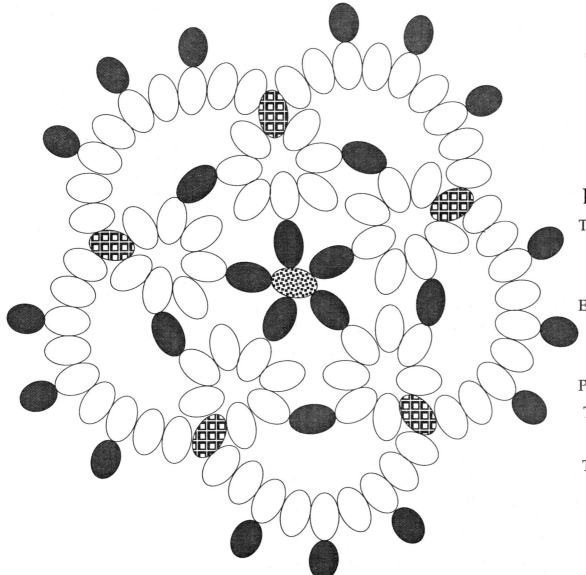

THIS IS ONE OF THE SIX, SMALL, SIDE MOTIFS THAT YOU WILL NEED FOR THIS HEART MEDALLION. DO NOT MAKE EACH ONE INDEPENDENTLY! **EVERY** SINGLE ONE CONNECTS TO EITHER ONE OF THE TWO, TOP, MEDIUM MOTIFS **OR** TO THE CENTER MOTIF. WE WILL DO EACH ONE IN TURN, MAKING THE CONNECTIONS AS WE GO. THIS ONE SHOWS A SPECIAL PURPOSE BEAD IN THE CENTER OF THE MOTIF, DESIGNATED BY THIS BEAD: THIS SPECIAL PURPOSE BEAD IS A BASE BEAD. THE CENTER "RING" OF THIS MOTIF IS FORMED BY CINCHING TOGETHER THE PICOTS OF THE LOOPS. THIS IS DONE *AFTER* THE FIVE, 8/3 LOOPS AND FIVE, 9/3 CHAINS ARE CONSTRUCTED. AFTER CINCHING IN THESE 5 PICOTS TO FORM THE CENTER "RING", SET A BASE BEAD INTO THE CENTER WITH A FIGURE '8' MOTION. YOU WILL NEED TO MANUALLY PUSH IT INTO THE SPACE—IT WILL FIT.

HERE IS THE HEART MEDALLION WITH ALL SIX OF THE SMALL MOTIFS IN PLACE AROUND THE LARGE CENTER AND THE TWO TOP MOTIFS. THE NEXT GRAPHICS WILL DEAL WITH EACH MOTIF IN TURN.

FIG. 16

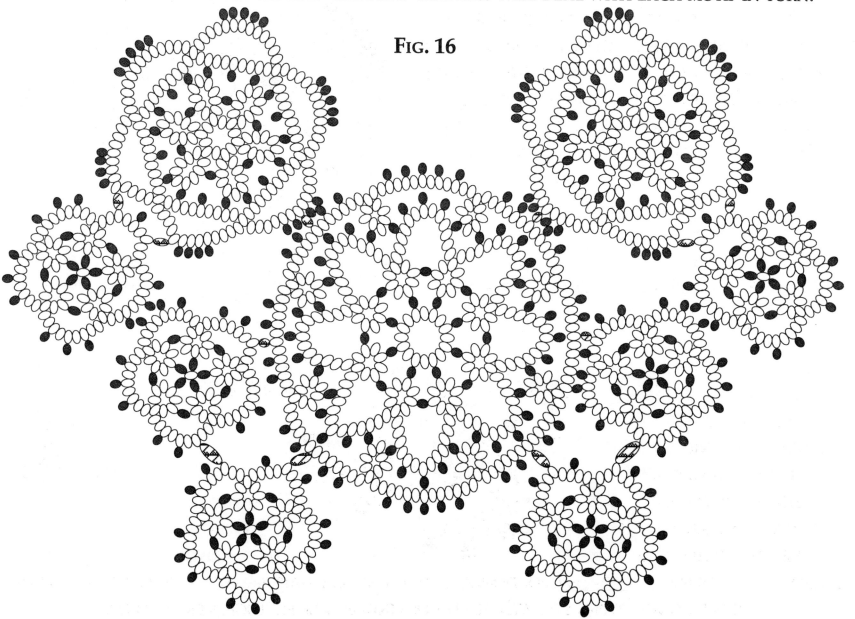

FIG. 17

THIS IS A CLOSE UP OF THE LEFT SIDE OF THE
MEDALLION, AND SHOWS HOW THE FIRST OF THE SIX,
SMALL, SIDE MOTIFS JOINS TO ONE OF THE TWO, TOP,
MEDIUM MOTIFS. WHEN YOU LOOK AT THESE
GRAPHICS, DO NOT CONCERN YOURSELF WITH THE
POSITION OF ANY OF THE GREY SHADED PICOTS IN
RELATION ONE TO ANOTHER. THE MOTIFS YOU ARE
JOINING TO ARE ALREADY ALL COMPLETE, AND THE
ONLY PICOTS WHICH ARE HANDLED DIFFERENTLY
ARE THE ONES WHICH JOIN THIS CURRENT
MOTIF, AND ARE HIGHLIGHTED AS
JOINING PICOTS. THE CONNECTIONS
MADE WILL LOOK PROPER IN THE
BEAD WORK. THE LACK OF
DIMENSION IN THESE
GRAPHICS OCCASIONALLY
REQUIRES AN UNREALISTIC
DISTORTION IN ORDER TO
SHOW THE PROPER
CONNECTIONS, AND THERE
ARE TIMES WHEN IT IS
LITERALLY IMPOSSIBLE TO SHOW PROPORTIONATELY WHAT REALLY HAPPENS. IF YOU WILL FOCUS ON THE
PROPER CONNECTIONS YOU WILL SEE IT DOES INDEED ALL FIT TOGETHER PROPERLY.

FIG. 18

HERE IS A CLOSE UP OF THE PLACEMENT OF THE
SECOND SMALL MOTIF. NOTICE THAT IT ONLY
CONNECTS TO THE CENTER MOTIF, AND NOT
TO THE SMALL MOTIF ABOVE IT.

I HAVE ALSO HIGHLIGHTED THE
CONNECTING PICOT BETWEEN THE TOP
MEDIUM MOTIF AND THE CENTER MOTIF
FOR CLARITY AND TO PROVIDE YOU
WITH A BETTER POINT OF
REFERENCE.

ALSO KEEP THIS IN MIND AS YOU
WORK, THIS HEART MEDALLION
HAS FILLER STRANDS AND UNTIL
THEY ARE IN PLACE, AND THEY GO
IN AT THE VERY END, THE
MEDALLION IS GOING TO BE FLOPPY
AND A BIT HARD TO MANAGE. YOU
WILL FIND THAT CROSS
REFERENCING WITH THE WRITTEN
INSTRUCTIONS CAN BE PARTICULARLY HELPFUL
NOW. IT IS TIMES LIKE THIS THAT YOU NEED TO
AVOID LOOKING AT THE LARGER PICTURE!
PATIENCE...

TOP, MEDIUM
MOTIF

THIS IS THE CLOSEUP OF THE
THIRD SMALL MOTIF ON THIS SIDE
OF THE CENTER MOTIF. THE
OTHER SIDE HAS ALL OF ITS
MOTIFS JOINED IN THE SAME
MANNER.

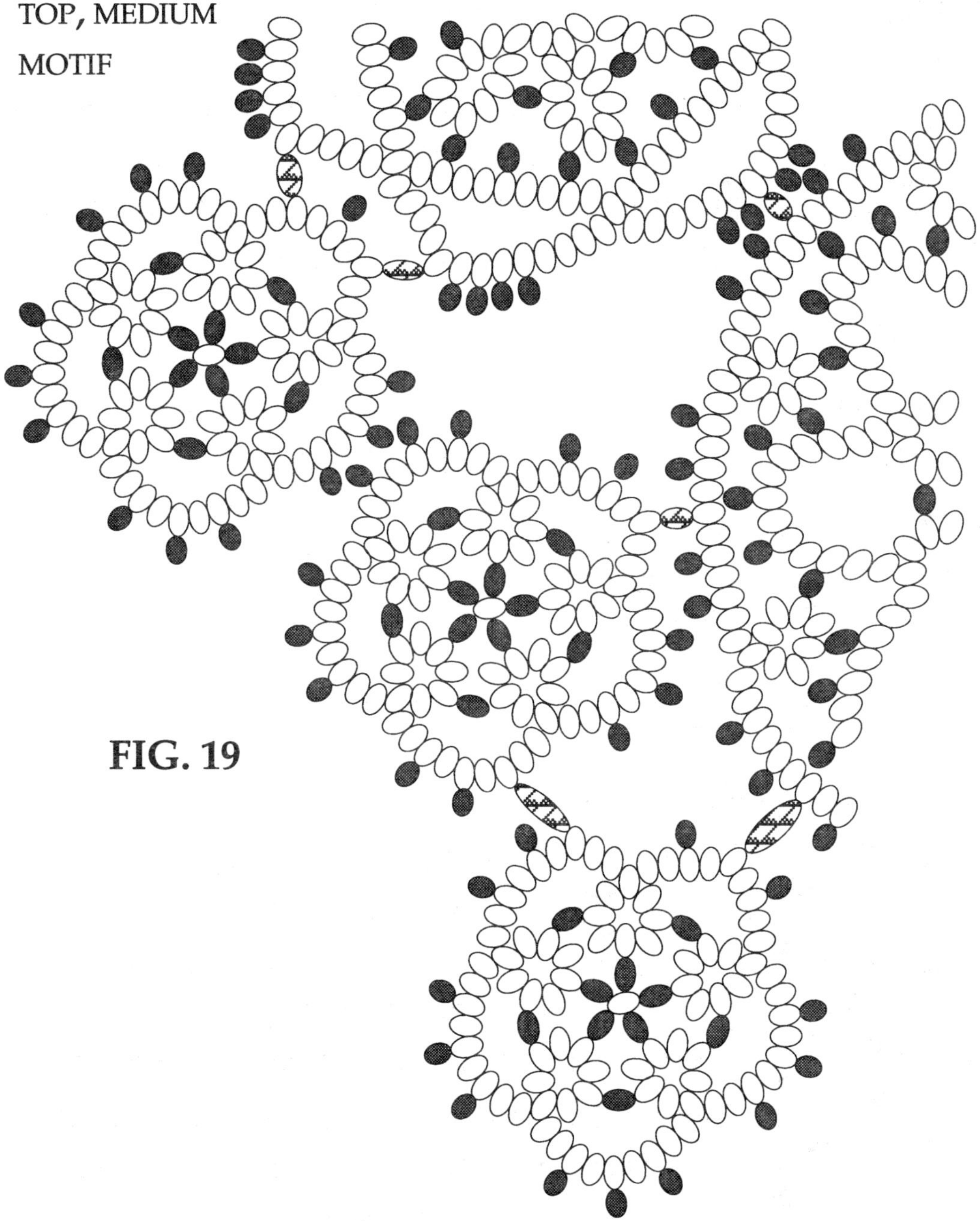

CENTER MOTIF

FIG. 19

FIG. 20

FIG. 21

THIS IS A CLOSE UP OF THE DOUBLE LOOP AND HOW IT CONNECTS TO THE CENTER MOTIF AND TO THE TWO, SMALL, BOTTOM MOTIFS. THE C/O BEADS OF THE DOUBLE LOOP, DESIGNATED BY THE C/O BEAD PATTERN OF WHICH YOU ARE BY NOW FAMILIAR, ARE JOINED TOGETHER IN THE SAME MANNER AS A PICOT IS MOUNTED UPON A BASE BEAD, AND AS WHEN JUMPING, IT IS A GOOD IDEA TO MAKE A COUPLE OF PASSES THROUGH TO CINCH THEM TOGETHER.

NOTICE THAT BECAUSE YOU ARE, IN EFFECT, JUMPING FROM ONE LOOP TO THE NEXT, ONE LOOP WILL BE DONE IN A CLOCKWISE FASHION AND ONE IN A COUNTERCLOCKWISE FASHION. FOR THIS REASON, THE LOOPS ARE NUMBERED, TO MAKE THE CONNECTIONS NOTED IN THE DIRECTIONS EASIER TO FOLLOW.

2ND SMALL SIDE MOTIF   CENTER MOTIF   2ND SMALL SIDE MOTIF

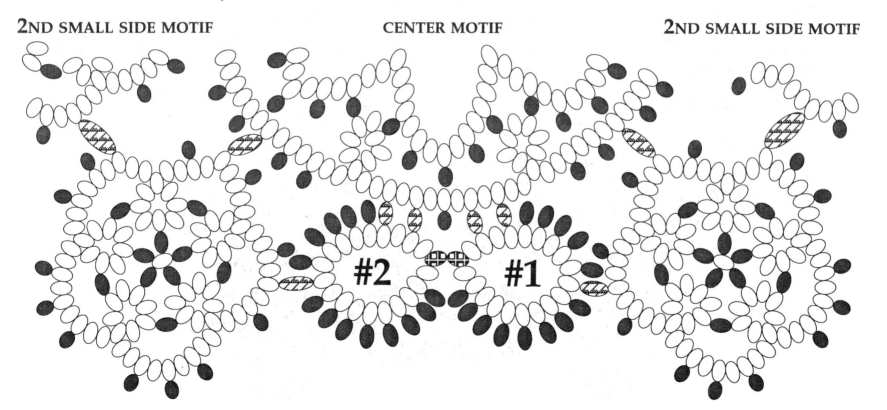

YOUR HEART MEDALLION SHOULD NOW LOOK LIKE THIS:

FIG. 22

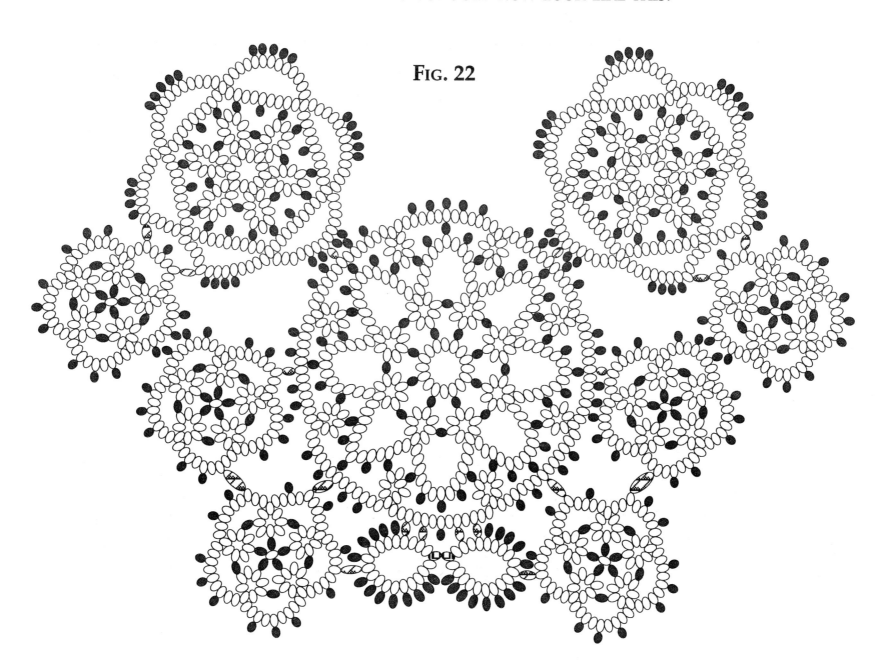

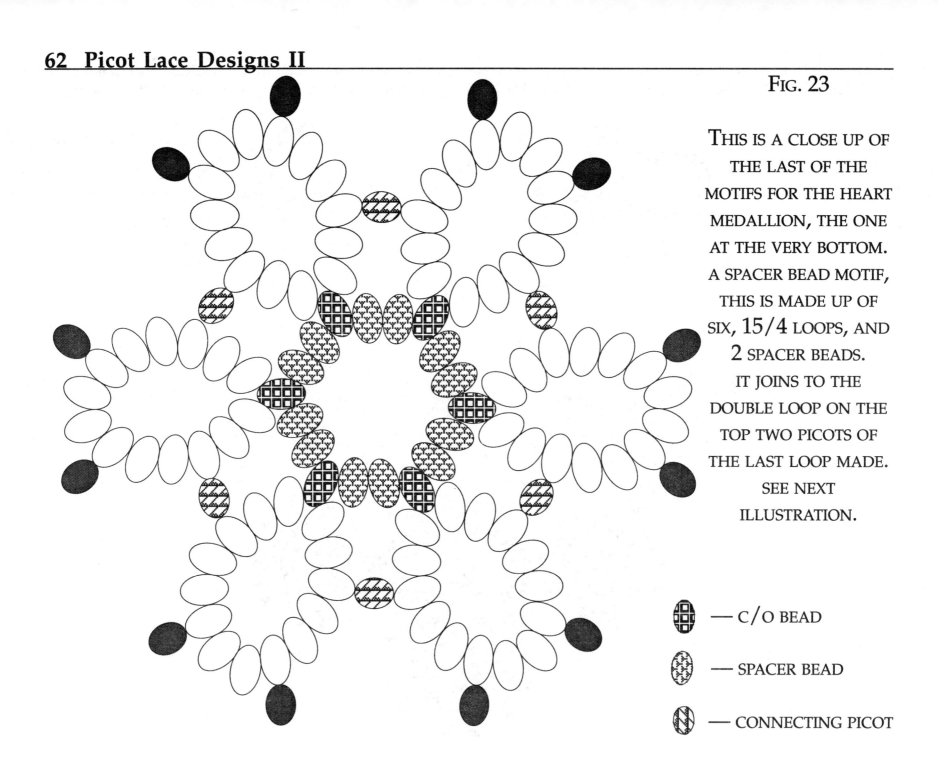

FIG. 23

THIS IS A CLOSE UP OF THE LAST OF THE MOTIFS FOR THE HEART MEDALLION, THE ONE AT THE VERY BOTTOM. A SPACER BEAD MOTIF, THIS IS MADE UP OF SIX, 15/4 LOOPS, AND 2 SPACER BEADS. IT JOINS TO THE DOUBLE LOOP ON THE TOP TWO PICOTS OF THE LAST LOOP MADE. SEE NEXT ILLUSTRATION.

— C/O BEAD

— SPACER BEAD

— CONNECTING PICOT

THE HEART MEDALLION IS NOW READY FOR THE FILLER STRANDS, AS THE LAST, BOTTOM MOTIF IS ADDED.

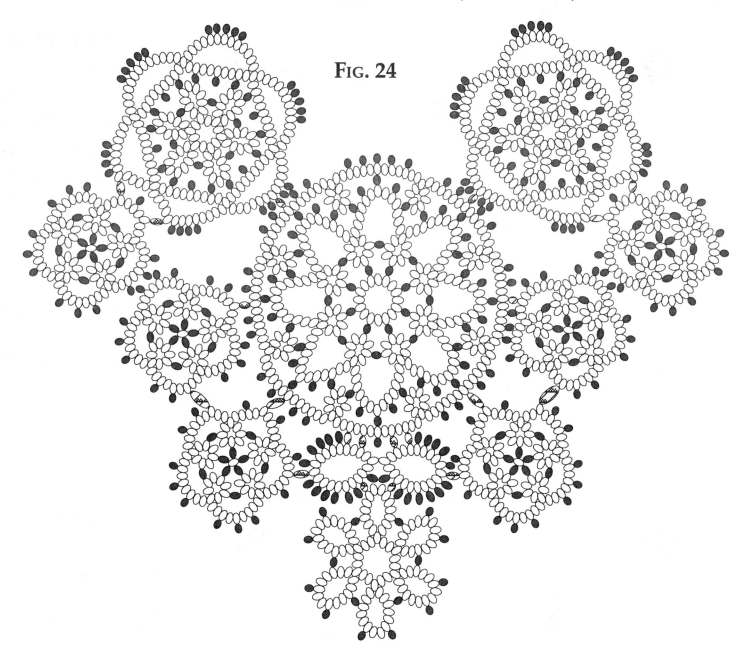

FIG. 24

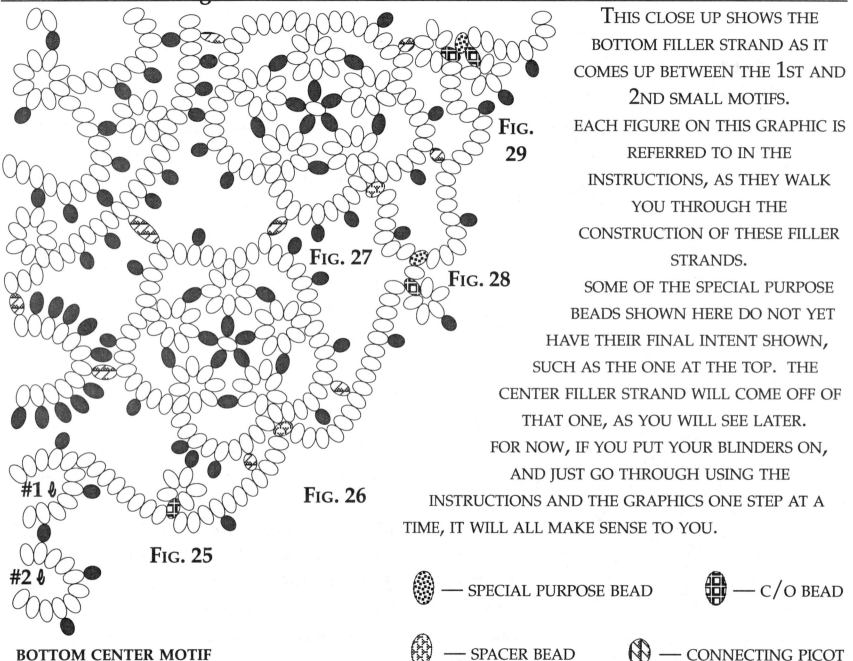

FIG.
29

FIG. 27

FIG. 28

FIG. 26

#1 ℓ

FIG. 25

#2 ℓ

BOTTOM CENTER MOTIF

THIS CLOSE UP SHOWS THE
BOTTOM FILLER STRAND AS IT
COMES UP BETWEEN THE 1ST AND
2ND SMALL MOTIFS.
EACH FIGURE ON THIS GRAPHIC IS
REFERRED TO IN THE
INSTRUCTIONS, AS THEY WALK
YOU THROUGH THE
CONSTRUCTION OF THESE FILLER
STRANDS.
SOME OF THE SPECIAL PURPOSE
BEADS SHOWN HERE DO NOT YET
HAVE THEIR FINAL INTENT SHOWN,
SUCH AS THE ONE AT THE TOP. THE
CENTER FILLER STRAND WILL COME OFF OF
THAT ONE, AS YOU WILL SEE LATER.
FOR NOW, IF YOU PUT YOUR BLINDERS ON,
AND JUST GO THROUGH USING THE
INSTRUCTIONS AND THE GRAPHICS ONE STEP AT A
TIME, IT WILL ALL MAKE SENSE TO YOU.

— SPECIAL PURPOSE BEAD   — C/O BEAD

— SPACER BEAD   — CONNECTING PICOT

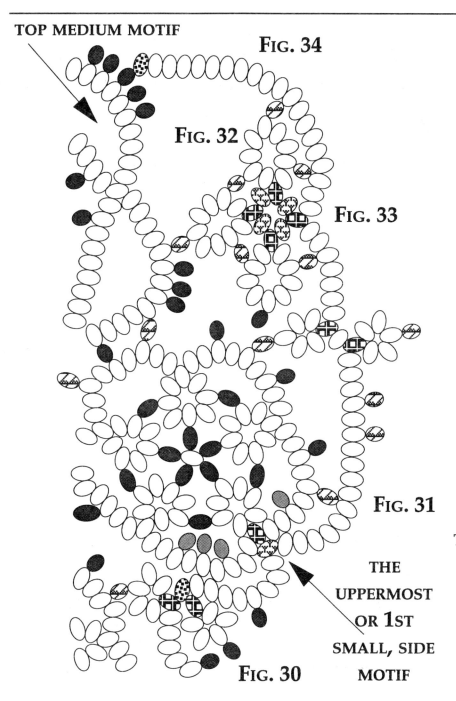

TOP MEDIUM MOTIF

FIG. 34

FIG. 32

FIG. 33

FIG. 31

FIG. 30

THE UPPERMOST OR 1ST SMALL, SIDE MOTIF

THIS IS THE CLOSE UP THAT PICKS UP WHERE THE LAST ONE LEFT OFF AND CONTINUES UP AROUND THE TOP EDGE.

FOR ORIENTATION PURPOSES, THE CONNECTING BEADS YOU USED PREVIOUSLY TO JOIN ONE MOTIF TO ANOTHER ARE STILL HIGHLIGHTED, BUT THEIR EDGES ARE GREY, WHEREAS THE CONNECTING BEADS YOU ARE PRESENTLY USING HAVE BLACK EDGES. ALSO, THE PICOTS WHICH ARE LIGHTLY SHADED ARE ONES ALREADY IN PLACE THAT I HAVE MOVED TO THE OTHER SIDE OF THE CHAIN FOR CLARITY SAKE—IN REALITY, THEY WILL REMAIN IN THEIR ORIGINAL POSITION.

AS IN THE LAST GRAPHIC, SOME OF THE SPECIAL PURPOSE BEADS ARE NOT BEING UTILIZED AS YET, BUT WILL BE. NOTICE, TOO, THAT SOME OF THE BEADS HIGHLIGHTED AS SPACER BEADS ARE NOT USED AS SUCH IN THE MORE CONVENTIONAL SENSE.

THE CONNECTING BEADS THAT SORT OF STICK OUT INTO NOWHERE ARE WHERE THE MEDALLION JOINS TO THIS HEART MEDALLION. SEE FIG. 44 FOR A CLOSE UP OF THIS CONNECTION PROCESS, WHICH WILL BE MADE AT THAT TIME.

THIS IS THE FILLER STRAND THAT COMES IN FROM BETWEEN THE 1ST AND 2ND SMALL, SIDE MOTIFS AND FILLS THE SPACE BETWEEN THEM AND THE CENTER MOTIF, AND UNDER THE TOP, MEDIUM MOTIF. USE THE C/O BEADS AND SPECIAL PURPOSE BEADS AS YOUR ORIENTATION POINT. IN TWO DIMENSIONS THERE WAS JUST NO WAY TO MAKE EVERYTHING FIT PROPERLY, BUT IN REALITY IT ALL DOES. JUST CONSTRUCT THE CHAIN AS INDICATED HERE AND IN THE DIRECTIONS. FOR VISUAL EASE, THE PRECONSTRUCTED MOTIF HAVE BEEN LIGHTENED EXCEPT FOR THE PERTINENT CONNECTION POINTS.

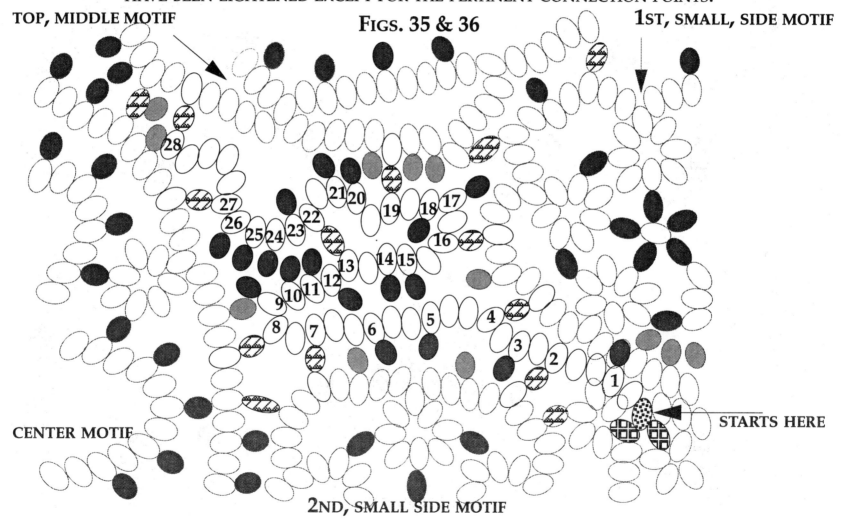

TOP, MIDDLE MOTIF

FIGS. 35 & 36

1ST, SMALL, SIDE MOTIF

CENTER MOTIF

STARTS HERE

2ND, SMALL SIDE MOTIF

These last two graphics show the two passes required to make this final filler strand. This first filler strand is the one at the very top that sits above the center spacer bead motif and between the two, top, medium, motifs. Here the beads highlighted as spacer beads are even less so in the conventional sense. The c/o beads in the center are just base beads in this pass, but as you will see, they will become c/o beads in the next pass. PS 6 and 12 will join to the next strand.

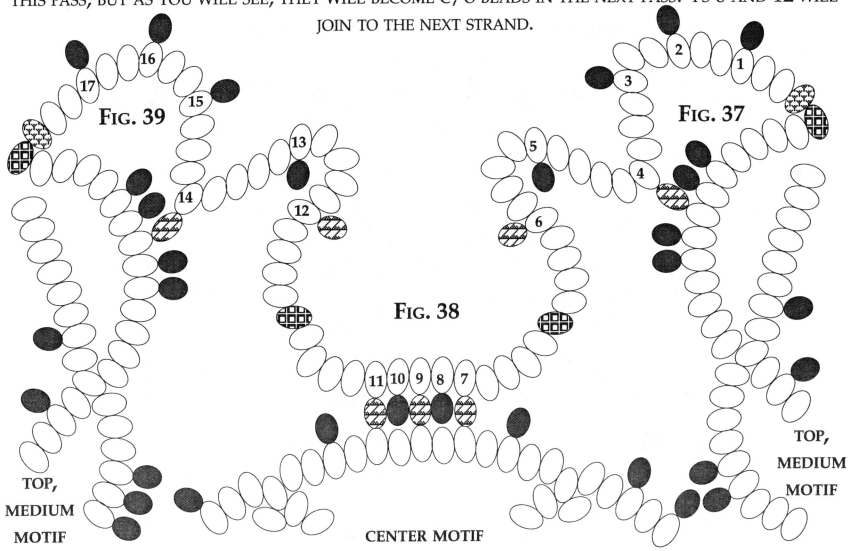

FIG. 39

FIG. 37

FIG. 38

TOP, MEDIUM MOTIF

TOP, MEDIUM MOTIF

CENTER MOTIF

YOU MADE IT! THIS GRAPHIC SHOWS BOTH PASSES OF THIS FINAL FILLER STRAND, AND ENUMERATES THE PICOTS FOR THE SECOND PASS. YOU CAN SEE THAT THE BASE BEADS HIGHLIGHTED AS C/O BEADS ARE NOW USED FOR THAT PURPOSE. THE SPECIAL PURPOSE BEADS ARE AT THE BEGINNING AND END, AND JOIN UP TO THEIR CONNECTING PICOTS AS IN A JUMP. AS YOU SEE, PS #1 AND #7 ARE NOT NEW, BUT JOIN TO THE PICOTS YOU MOUNTED IN YOUR FIRST PASS, WHICH WERE DESIGNATED AS CONNECTING PICOTS. COMPARE PAGES 67 AND 68 FOR CLARITY.

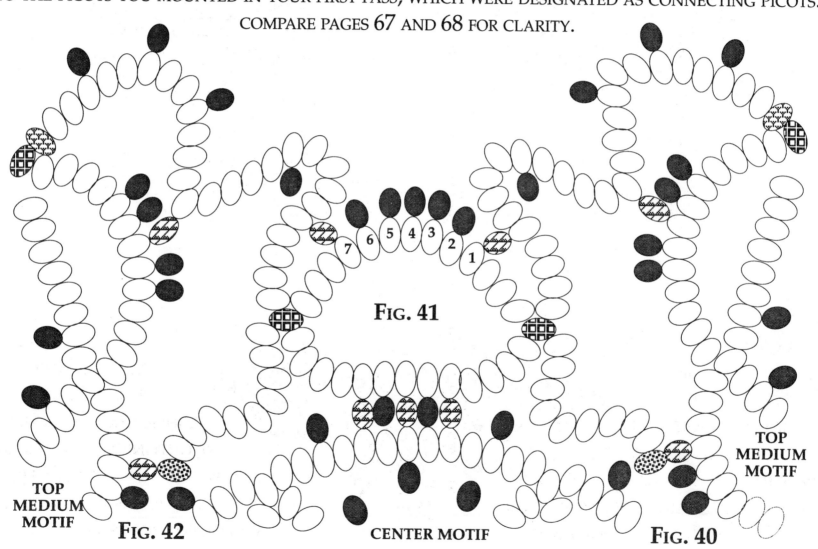

FIG. 41

TOP MEDIUM MOTIF

TOP MEDIUM MOTIF

FIG. 42

CENTER MOTIF

FIG. 40

IN THIS GRAPHIC, I HAVE LEFT THE CONNECTING PICOTS OF THE FILLER STRANDS HIGHLIGHTED TO GIVE YOU AN OVERVIEW OF THE FILLER STRANDS AND HOW THEY FIT INTO THE WHOLE.

FIG. 43

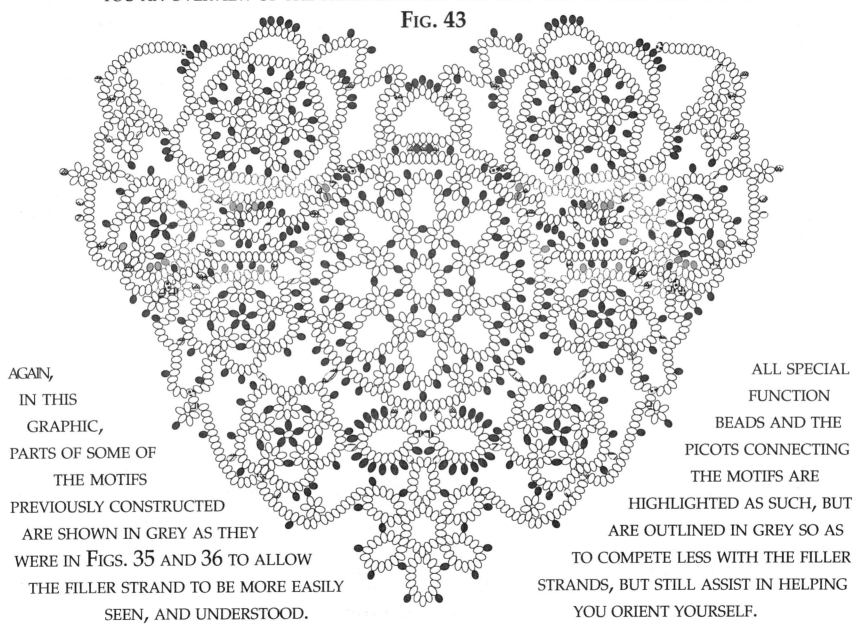

AGAIN, IN THIS GRAPHIC, PARTS OF SOME OF THE MOTIFS PREVIOUSLY CONSTRUCTED ARE SHOWN IN GREY AS THEY WERE IN FIGS. 35 AND 36 TO ALLOW THE FILLER STRAND TO BE MORE EASILY SEEN, AND UNDERSTOOD.

ALL SPECIAL FUNCTION BEADS AND THE PICOTS CONNECTING THE MOTIFS ARE HIGHLIGHTED AS SUCH, BUT ARE OUTLINED IN GREY SO AS TO COMPETE LESS WITH THE FILLER STRANDS, BUT STILL ASSIST IN HELPING YOU ORIENT YOURSELF.

FIG. 44

THE NEW (AND LAST) CHAIN AND
LOOP

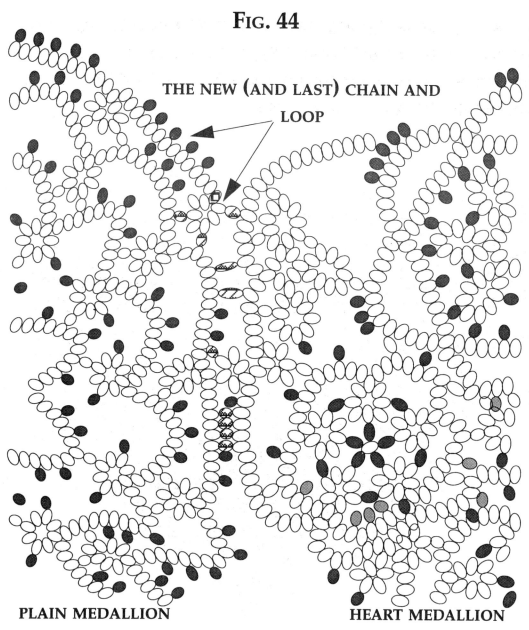

PLAIN MEDALLION   **HEART MEDALLION**

THIS CLOSE UP IS OF THE CONNECTION
OF THE HEART MEDALLION TO THE
NEIGHBORING PLAIN MEDALLIONS. THE
PLAIN MEDALLION HAS AN ADDITIONAL
13/5 CHAIN AND 8/3 LOOP ADDED,
THE LOOP LOCKING INTO THE CHAIN
ON THE HEART MEDALLION AS WELL AS
TO THE LAST ROW OF THE PLAIN
MEDALLION, AS SHOWN HERE.
I RECOMMEND SETTING A NEW THREAD
ONTO THE EDGE AND THEN ADDING
THIS LAST CHAIN FIRST, THEN THE
LOOP, THEN JUMPING OUT OF THE NEW
LOOP AND INTO THE CHAIN
BELONGING TO THE 2ND ROW OF THE
PLAIN MEDALLION. THIS WILL ENABLE
YOU TO TRAVEL DOWN, MAKING THOSE
CONNECTIONS. THEN JUMP OVER TO
THE HEART MEDALLION AND COME
BACK UP, MAKING THOSE ADDITIONAL
CONNECTIONS EASIEST DONE FROM
THAT SIDE. THIS WILL MAKE THIS
IMPORTANT JUNCTION STRONGER AND
BE THE EASIEST WAY TO MAKE THE
NECESSARY CONNECTIONS.

FIG. 45

THIS GRAPHIC SHOWS THE FINISHED PLAIN AND HEART MEDALLIONS CONNECTED TO ONE ANOTHER. YOU WILL NOTICE THAT THE PLAIN MEDALLION RISES AT AN ANGLE UP FROM THE HEART MEDALLION, THIS IS AS IT NEEDS TO BE TO SIT PROPERLY AS A COLLAR, OF WHATEVER SIZE YOU CHOOSE TO MAKE IT, OFF THE SHOULDER LIKE MINE, OR SMALLER.

This dew drop collar has been the most ambitious collar I have graphed out to date, as evidenced by the 45 graphics it took to represent it. I will continue to graph out and publish picot lace designs, and look forward to introducing you all to more and more complex techniques as new territory is covered in picot lace designs. Use this space for notations of your own regarding color combinations that work for you, and please feel free to send in your comments for addition to the picot lace newsletter. I thank you for your encouragment and support for this new form of beadwork. Enjoy the rhythm!

NOTES